Discov

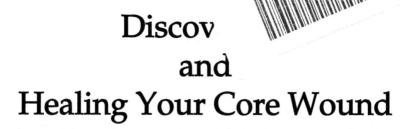

and
Healing Your Core Wound

by

Paul Sequoia Rauch

ISBN: 979-8-89504-943-3

Non-fiction

Discovering and Healing Your Core Wound©

Copyright at Library of Congress Cataloging-In-Publication Data.

To all those who choose to heal.

Contents

INTRODUCTION

Discovering and Healing Your Core Wound explains how to recognize and heal your own specific Core Wound. As we all have only one Core Wound, identifying it shows you exactly what to focus on to heal yourself. It is a very practical and simple process yet also very life changing.

Our Core Wound is where all our issues spring from; it is the deepest cause. The discovery of our Core Wound unlocks an awareness within us of our own internal code, which then allows accelerated healing to take place and lasts for life when we fully understand it. It's easier than one might think, and it's all spelled out in this book.

All of our issues spring from our Core Wound.

Additionally, the people of our primary relationships who also choose to discover and heal their Core Wound greatly increases our ability to help each other heal and create more love, fun, and consciousness together. The deepest question we could ask to get to understand and heal with someone we love is, "What's your Core Wound?" Knowing that, we could then help one another heal our most reactive pain and end all the self-limiting lies we all tell ourselves - lies that limit our joy, our purpose in life, and the various forms of true intimacy and love we could have.

Further still, in order to unveil our higher purpose in life, a critical part of our healing must be to let go of our small story of personal woe, which is directly connected to our Core Wound. Healing our Core Wound sets us free, free to start living our greater purpose in life; free of the Wound that holds us back in any way; and free to heal mentally, emotionally, spiritually, and physically, because it's all connected.

Healing our Core Wound is about consciously creating our own reality, first leading to a healthy inner world and on to a healthy outer world with healthy relationships.

Healing does not have to be difficult or painful. My healing has been a blast, especially topped off with the rewards. There was no pathway for me, but I've pioneered and trailblazed a map for you. I've done the work and the long division for you. After all the healing I've both received and conducted for over thirty years, I discovered my Core Wound last; instead, you can address your Core Wound first and avoid up to decades of slower or actually ineffective means of healing. Otherwise, you're free to have dysfunctional, unfulfilling relationships; wallow around in the throes of your Core Wound; take your anti-depressants or whatever; be like a rudderless sailboat powerlessly reacting to the chaotic winds on an ocean of personal anxiety and worldly drama; be in some fake state of "joy," which is often merely based on some deeply rooted amount of denial; be angry or a victim all your life; never know your true purpose in life; or be in any other compromised state of living.

My healing expedition began in the mid-1980s, so *Discovering and Healing your Core Wound* is the result of over three decades of personal experience and development in both healing myself then transitioning into counseling a large variety of clients. Healing became a lifestyle, and mutually sharing what worked with other like-minded people who were committed to healing just evolved naturally. My healing matured over time and led me to becoming a counselor; for over twenty years I have now counseled thousands of clients, including individuals, couples, families, and groups. My life has transformed me into becoming a specialist Core Wound Counselor©.

If you've never heard of Core Wound Counselor© or Core Wound Coach©, it's because this is ground-breaking, original work. I've learned this not from text books in class, but from the synergy of my own life experience of healing. I've embraced all kinds of uncommon healing, from phenomenal non-traditional doctors, very powerful five-day emotional-release workshops, elite metaphysical seminars, deep herbal healing of my internal organs, and so much more. All of this worked extraordinarily well and was far outside of mainstream awareness. As deep and as vital as my healing has been, it has been so rewarding and fun that I'm never going to stop. The real pain is in not healing.

The real pain is in not healing.

I've also spent a large amount of my life in nature ever since I was three years old. Mother nature always consoled me when I needed it, taught me, healed me, and has always put me in some level of joy. That said, I have had the ideal venue to work in. My current "office" is in the beautiful scenic forests of Sedona, Arizona, in which I do my professional counseling.

In 2002 a new spiritual retreat company began in Sedona, and, along with other very high awards, became one of the top eleven spiritual retreats in the entire world in 2021.[1] On reputation alone and without a job application nor even an interview, the owner hired me as one of a handful of counselors, coaches, and practitioners to start the company, and I have now given over twelve years of counseling through this very successful company (though starting in 2002, I had a hiatus for a few years out of state to take care of my grandma and more). It has provided me the platform which has allowed me to develop my brand of counseling, and I have acquired hundreds of remarkable testimonials.

I have met and successfully counseled a wide variety of people from several countries now, from two different multi-ten-billionaire couples to people going into debt to get here; from famous entertainers, the wife of a European ambassador to the U.S., and Fortune 500 CEOs to people dealing with deaths, sexual abuse, and infidelity; from people in their pre-teens to those in their eighties; from people of all races, origin, sexual orientation, and stories. All of them make for the most remarkable puzzles, and I become immersed with solving them. As an avid and curious life-long student of life and human nature, the uniqueness of all my clients fascinates me, and I have found that everyone has a Core Wound. Many have focused on and beautifully succeeded in becoming wealthy, yet many are very unhappy because their unhealed Core Wound is still controlling the inner and reactionary world of their lives.

Everyone has a Core Wound.

For each of us, our Core Wound developed out of our childhood, and my childhood forced me into having to do more healing than most. Born in a metaphorical mosh pit, my upbringing gave me the deepest Wound of all, a Wound that many don't even survive, and I barely did.

A mosh pit is a rowdy place where the audience takes over the dance-floor area in front of a live "emo" band (very aggressive music and screaming vocals), a crowded, messy place where most are sloppy drunk, rowdy, careless, and where some of their lowest nature comes out. The metaphor fits my being just a little kid, the youngest, with two very alcoholic parents; an extremely unhappy, rageful mother; a ceaselessly cruel brother and his equally cruel older neighbor friend; and being completely unprotected with no one looking out for me. There was no love in our family of four; in fact, the word love was never even spoken nor displayed – no hugs and no affection amongst anyone, but rather quite the opposite.

At thirty, my unhealed childhood finally caught up with me, and it left me with no choice but to heal or die. At age twelve I had begun drinking; it became almost daily at fourteen. My best friend died from alcoholism just forty-five days shy of thirty-three. Born ten days apart in the same neighborhood, we met in first grade at five years old, and our lives paralleled one another like twin souls. If I hadn't chosen to heal, I would have shared the same fate as him. At fifty-seven, my mom died of alcoholism twenty-three days after he did. With no doubt, both of their Core Wounds actually killed them; this is why our Core Wound is not to be minimized as a core belief (more on that later) nor misdiagnosed.

My reawakening began at thirty when I met my Inner Child, which completely changed the course of my life. Since that turning point, with plenty of help that came my way, my healing of at least three-dozen major issues came to pass, and they all boiled down to my Core Wound; I discovered that it supported and caused them all. My life of healing first began physically then emotionally then mentally, and throughout it all, spiritually. I found that what ultimately matters most is to heal our Core Wound. It makes sense of everything. As one client said, "It's the one problem that solves a hundred."

I might as well tell you of four big things I've healed that the experts will say can't be true: that a three-year-old can consciously think of committing suicide; that one's eyes can permanently change from dark brown to hazel/blue in one's thirties; that the completion of one's physical growth can't happen in one's thirties (that's how compromised my endocrine system was by drinking so early in life and how the chronic stress of Adverse Childhood Experiences affects our physical growth and health, proven in a genius doctor's pioneering, must-read book[2]); and that RAD syndrome (Reactive Attachment Disorder) cannot be healed. I'm proof it can all be done.

My path also led me to college much later than normal, and I earned four degrees in thirty-three consecutive months, all summa cum laude, plus won a huge achievement award for it from the governor of the State of Washington. After that, I finally felt and proved to myself that I was whole, undamaged, and alive and well in spirit, body, mind and emotion for the first time in my life. Above all, I felt incredibly grateful and relieved.

All this is simply to say I come with the qualifications to show how to heal our Core Wound. I'm living proof that anybody can heal and even thrive with joy. I've tackled some heavy stuff, so if I can do it anyone can do it. Anyone who so desires can enjoy the life-changing benefits from such healing. One just has to want to and stay conscious of doing so.

To heal one's Core Wound one only has to stay conscious and willing enough to do so.

I had a lot more healing to do than most, and a lot of my energy was taken up by just having to survive and focus on it. My greatest accomplishment may be in having made it from being a very abused (in all four ways), despairing little boy to attaining an undying *joie de vivre*. Nothing's worth losing that. That is my own personal miracle. You can also have yours.

I never thought I'd find such mirth in what I went through. Eventually you'll be able to laugh about your Core Wound because of the ridiculous lie it is, rather than always being triggered by it and letting it run and ruin your life. I laugh a lot now, even about all the life-threatening abuse of my first three decades of life, especially my first decade, it's so beyond the pale. And I now know the greatest joy is the joy of healing.

The greatest joy is the joy of healing.

My life has been one of a humble and uncommon triumph, far transcendent of my old small story of pain. Somebody had to go through it, somebody who would be willing to make something out of what I went through and who would find gratitude, purpose, and fulfillment in doing so. It is with this intent I extend this offer of healing to you; it's your choice. Who better to offer it than someone who has come out of the mosh-pit to have survived and healed the worst of Core Wounds?

Vulneratus non Victus, a motto a great young client had tattooed on her arm, translates as "Wounded but not Conquered." We all have our scars and wounds, especially our Core Wound, and that Wound can be healed. We need not be conquered nor compromised by it.

CHAPTER 1
TAKING YOUR "X-RAY"

*"Like an organic computer, your brain has an operating system –
a series of rules that organizes and defines all of the chaotic input
that flows in all day long.... In fact, it is the very programming of
your brain's operating system that defines your perception of
reality."* Dan Brown[3]

As mentioned in the introduction, the concept of a Core Wound has largely been unheard of, unrecognized, and at best misunderstood or minimized as a core belief. However, our Core Wound is much more than a belief. That more is what I call the "Twelve": our thoughts, emotions, attitude, beliefs, desire, imagination, expectation, behavior, choices, perspective, dreams, and will. The "Twelve" of our Core Wound affects our mental, emotional, physical, and spiritual health. Our "Twelve" are not just components that determine our internal reality or self-image, they are more the synergistic resonance of our being. I've placed "Twelve" in quote marks because it symbolizes being more than just that. It is what we emanate, as if we are "wearing" our Wound as our identity; thus, it is also what we create and attract in our lives. All of the "Twelve" are affected by our Core Wound, so when we heal our Core Wound, our "Twelve" all change as well and thus our resonance, our attractor.

All of our "Twelve" are affected by our Core Wound.

As one example that our Core Wound is much more than a belief, my Core Wound caused me to have heart disease. My Core Wound literally caused my heart to be wounded. It was not genetic, nor was it caused by a mere belief. Rheumatic fever is known as inflammation in and of the heart. Starting at age eight I was sick with it for two years before my parents ever took me to a doctor to have it discovered. (Compare that to people who take their pets to the vet within *the first hours* of sickness). By then I had full-on heart disease at age ten; my heart beat three times per beat instead of twice and pumped severely anemic blood that was actually orange and almost as thin as water. It took two more years to recover. I am very fortunate to say that my heart disease and anemia were eventually fully healed. However, the entire ordeal took one-third of my childhood and included five months in bed at age ten/eleven. I realize now that my Core Wound, "No one cares," which started long before my rheumatic fever, permeated all of my "Twelve." By age three, I remember already being heartbroken from all the abuse and uncaring from the family my Soul chose to be born to. I say this only to point out that our Core Wound is much more than a core belief; we actually get wounded, and that wound is at least psychological and emotional if not also physical and spiritual.

Yes, I ultimately chose to believe I have a Soul, and that it chose the family I was born to. As with any belief, it can't be proven. That's precisely the difference between a belief and the Core Wound; a belief is not a fact, but a wound is, such as having heart disease. The point is, since a belief can't be proven, we can consciously choose beliefs that empower us with purpose and destiny rather than, like I first did, believe I would forever be a victim of my family of origin and thus wallow in self-pity, depression, and rage. With commitment and attention, I healed all that out of me, and it all came from my Core Wound. In believing I am a Soul who chose to be born to the people who wounded me, I empowered myself to have it mean something, to have a reason, a purpose, and I have since made it part of my destiny of healing. It also allowed me to forgive and even thank my parents and brother (via "independent resolution," which is doing it without them since they were either deceased or unavailable) for doing such a great job of giving me my Core Wound so I could finally heal it – even on a Soul level.

With that said, enough has now been added to the introduction to simply begin the process of discovering and healing your Core Wound.

First Step

At the top of a piece of paper, write down the people who influenced you the most up until you were age eleven. Names are not necessary but can be used. This includes anyone that raised you and those that didn't technically raise you but influenced your childhood in a big way, good or bad. In my case, I only have mom, dad, my brother (almost four years older) and his older neighbor-friend, Dick. I've had clients who only had mom to others having aunts, stepfathers, stepmothers, uncles, grandparents, or maybe a cousin. On rare occasions it might include some people outside the family such as a neighbor, coach, pastor or teacher, etc. If you had a biological father or mother who left you - even if you were too young to remember, but you knew about it before you were twelve - they must go in there, too. Occasionally I allow some to include church, but only if it was as influential as a "person." We're really only looking for the influence of people, not institutions, and we don't have to dig too deep; we're only looking for the big stuff, the stuff that stands out the most that you remember when you were growing up.

Once you do that part then write a list of ten good traits and ten bad traits of all those people as if they were one person. Just "put them in a big brown bag and shake it up" and see what the biggest traits are that come out of it. They don't have to have any of the traits in common.

Even the same person could have conflicting traits, such as kind and mean, let alone the mix of others.

For some examples, there are several common traits a lot of people grew up with, such as angry, loving, hard-working, alcoholic, supportive, adventurous, sense of humor, critical, resigned, upbeat, depressed, codependent, and so on. Sometimes I have to push people to get ten on either side, but you also don't have to stop at ten if there's more. I've continued to stay with the process and now have twenty-six on the bad and finally relented to get fifteen on the good, some of which I didn't really want to admit. Some of you might not want to admit there was anything bad, and some of you might not want to admit there was much of anything good. No one is the same, and there's no judgment about this. The point is to be fully honest on both sides. It is what it is; it's just the traits of those who influenced your childhood the most.

Mom   Dad   Stepdad   Aunt Ester   Grandparents   Brother

GOOD	BAD
Provider	Alcoholic
Optimistic	Abusive (Men. Emo. Phy. Sex)
Caring	Bad Communicator
Good Cook	Depressed
Intelligent	Unprotective
Creative	Unfair
Hard Worker	Mean
Loyal	Shaming
Honest	Critical
Resourceful	Abandoning

***

I imagine you have that urge to just keep reading, but in order to get the most out of this, please stop and do this process first. This book is one of process, not a story to be read through like most books. Take your time with this step. Your ego is the one that wants to keep going; you will find that it is part of your ego that you need to heal the most.

Now I'll introduce the main actors within you that are playing out the story of your life:

1. Your reactive, programmed Subconscious

2. Your Conscious Self, miniscule and far less active than the subconscious, but more powerful when its power of choice is used.
3. Your Inner Child, which is still very much alive within you psychologically and emotionally. It is that part of you which existed from birth to eleven years old when the "Twelve" of your Core Wound was formed in your subconscious and unconscious.
4. Your Negative Ego, the worst enemy in your life and the subconscious voice of your Core Wound.
5. Your Will, the emotional, psychological, and creative willpower which can bond with your Conscious Self.
6. Your Future Self.
7. Your Higher Self and/or Soul (I experience them as different, but you can choose).

I bring this up now mostly to introduce the Negative Ego. Your Negative Ego thinks it knows everything, especially that you don't have to follow the rules, especially when it starts to suspect – or knows – that it's going to get busted. It thinks it knows what's best for you and has been in control all your life; it's like an addict that cares more about itself than for the wellbeing of you as a whole. It is a know-it-all and is your biggest saboteur, your Negative Ego.

So, STOP here and do the process of the First Step. It's easy and only takes about ten minutes, give or take, but take as long as you need. Introspect your childhood and feel and think about it as deeply as you can. This is the only part of this book where I encourage you to stop to do this one process.

Second Step

You don't have to stop at ten traits on each side, or, if you got stuck before you got to ten, here are some suggestions to help you add to or complete your First Step worksheet: talented, popular, social, athletic, outdoorsy, intelligent, provider, good cook, artsy/craftsy, moral, friendly, honorable, trusting, optimistic, fun, resourceful, adventurous, nature-lover, animal-lover, people pleaser, vivacious, protective, fair, nonjudgmental, creative, artistic, sweet, understanding, compassionate, good communicator, present, honest, trustable, reliable, family oriented, affectionate, curious; furious, rageful, depressed, lonely, martyr, addicted, abusive (mental, emotional, physical, sexual), liar, boring, betraying, unfaithful, unpredictable, punishing, unprotective, unloving, dismissive, despairing, torturer, apathetic, non-present (mentally, emotionally, physically), chauvinistic (male or female), unsupportive, cruel, unaffectionate, secretive, violent, oversensitive, repressed, unapologetic, neglectful, reclusive, controlling, bullying, unforgiving, manipulative, narcissistic, selfish, attachment disorder, bad communicator, vengeful, unfair, critical, shaming, guilt inducing, scary, anxious, fearful. Give it some thought again, you may have ones not mentioned. I always hear new ones.

When you're complete with filling out the traits, in the space between the people that influenced your childhood and the lists of their good and bad traits, draw an arrow pointing down. Also, at the bottom of the page underneath all the traits, write: Subconscious.

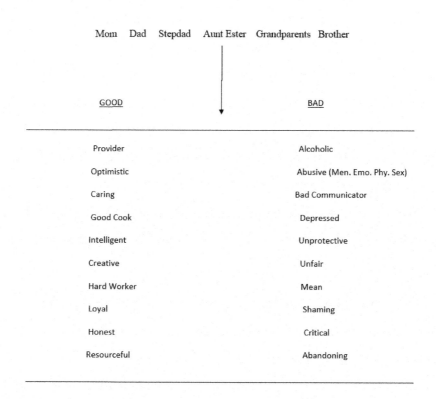

Mom   Dad   Stepdad   Aunt Ester   Grandparents   Brother

GOOD   BAD

Provider	Alcoholic
Optimistic	Abusive (Men. Emo. Phy. Sex)
Caring	Bad Communicator
Good Cook	Depressed
Intelligent	Unprotective
Creative	Unfair
Hard Worker	Mean
Loyal	Shaming
Honest	Critical
Resourceful	Abandoning

Subconscious

This is simply to show that the people who most influenced your childhood downloaded their traits into your subconscious. These are the main traits that programmed your subconscious, which is like what the operating system (OS) is to a computer. I call this confluence of traits the Inner Child's Operating System, the ICOS. You could also call it the Template which determines the pattern of your life. The ICOS is why some patterns keep getting repeated over and over that we don't even want; this is because our subconscious is running the show. These are like non-deletable files that automatically run the "Twelve" as an autonomous, reactionary psychological/emotional system. It could also be called your emotional and psychological blueprint. All those traits are what influenced your "Twelve" when you were most susceptible and vulnerable.

You can think of it as metaphorically similar to the ability of our autonomous nervous system running the functions of our body automatically such as heartbeat, breathing, sweating, and a myriad of other things. Our subconscious automatically runs our psychological/emotional being (by default) until consciously overridden like debugging a computer.

How we were raised, influenced, and programmed is literally how the neuropathways of our brain got connected (or not connected), which formed our "Twelve." Our entire nervous system literally got programmed with our Core Wound, so healing our Core Wound will actually change the neuropathways of our brain and our nervous system, now known as neuroplasticity.

Our Core Wound (CW) developed out of a combination of the inherited psychological, emotional, and behavioral traits, both good and bad, that were transferred into us like "psychological/emotional DNA" from the collective of people that influenced our childhood the most. The combination of all those traits created our version of normal, which also became our comfort zone even if it was an abusive environment. It's also known as our "familiar" (from the word, family). Knowing that this became our familiar, our comfort zone, and what we consider to be normal is key to understanding our Core Wound.

Understanding what was normal, our comfort zone, or our familiar is key to understanding our Core Wound.

For instance, if abuse was normal, it's likely it became more expected or accepted as we grew older, even subconsciously desired in some form because we resonate with it. We have Velcro with it. The same is true for those who were one of the one percent or less who grew up with someone having unconditional love as a trait.

The most important thing to know so far is that our subconscious has no power to choose, so it can't choose to be different on its own. This is because it is not conscious enough to make such choice. The subconscious cannot change on its own. The subconscious runs on automatic and is solely reactionary. Basically, it can only react according to the "Twelve" that developed as its programming. Its job is to maintain the status quo at all costs.

Our subconscious has no ability to consciously choose to be different.

***

Third Step

Now that you've filled out the traits, the next step is to checkmark all the traits on the good side that you see in your most significant partner or ex-partner (sexual partner) ever since you've known them. This is why you were attracted to them in the first place because they probably – hopefully - have most of the traits you loved growing up with as a kid that became your normal, which is what you resonate with. You can put a percentage next to this side of the circle for the number of checkmarks you have such as sixty percent for six out of ten.

Now do the same thing on the bad side. You may be equally attracted to the bad traits because of your subconscious comfort zone or ICOS "Twelve" that draw in the close relationships you resonate with. The traits that are checked on this side are where you still need healing the most. Mostly, you married a version of your mother and father and a combination of all of the people you wrote at the top of your "x-ray" page in order to heal those issues (traits) they taught and gave you. Your partner or ex is or was mirroring to you what you didn't like when you were a child; they are your own unhealed issues you'd probably rather blame your partner for having, rather than take responsibility for those being your own issues you need to heal within yourself, and those issues most likely cause you to get "triggered" or react the most.

You can use two major relationships if you want to go deeper; this way you can see how you have improved or not, and I recommend that you do so. This way you can see what traits overlap and are repeated or mirrored back to you throughout your life. You may have some issues that are tripled: you didn't like them growing up, and you may have had two partners that have those same traits that have provoked those same issues.

Once you heal your Core Wound, and thus these issues within yourself, one way or another these issues will be healed enough to either no longer bother you or not even be in your life. Believe me, if I can do it, you can do it. Imagine not getting triggered anymore! What would you do with all the freed-up energy? Maybe consciously create what you've always wanted?

Do yourself a favor and pause here just to fully finish this process before you read on. You may even want to let this incubate within you and allow a little time to let ideas percolate up from your subconscious memory. The more thorough you are, the more accurate your Core Wound discovery will be; it is a combination of both sides, good and bad, but the Wound came from the bad side, perhaps eased by the good. The negative traits are all shared causes of your Core Wound. It is important to get this right because your Core Wound is with you for life, but the good news is it will be inactivated when you do the rest of the processes thoroughly.

Mom   Dad   Stepdad   Aunt Ester   Grandparents   Brother

GOOD   BAD

GOOD		BAD	
Provider	X	Alcoholic	X √ (3x)
Optimistic		Abusive (Ment/Emo/Phy/Sex)	X √ (3x)
Caring	√	Bad Communicator	X √ (3x)
Good Cook	√	Depressed	X
Intelligent	X √	Unprotective	X
Creative	√	Unfair	
Hard Worker	X √	Mean	X
Loyal	X	Shaming	√
Honest	√	Critical	X √ (3x)
Resourceful		Abandoning	X √ (3x)

X = 40% √ = 60%   X = 80% √ = 60%

Subconscious

31

For the Fictitious Character (FC) used for the example of filling out the diagram above, X represents the ex, and ex had forty percent of the traits FC loved in their childhood from the people that influenced them the most (not that great and a beginning indicator of FC's Core Wound). The checkmark represents FC's current or more recent partner, and that partner has sixty percent on the good side (a twenty percent improvement).

On the bad side, FC's ex had eighty percent of the traits FC grew up with, and FC's current or most recent partner had/has sixty percent, a twenty percent improvement. However, five of the traits overlap, which are the more poignant issues FC has had to deal with that were programmed into him or her and cause them to be triggered. These issues are the five that have been with FC all their life; FC didn't like them growing up, and especially hasn't liked them in FC's two main lover/partnerships, so they have been manifested at least three major times. It is FC's subconscious that has drawn them into his/her life (maintaining what is normal and familiar), and it shows FC where he/she most needs healing. It's possible FC also has those same five traits within themselves as reactive behaviors, too, since they were also subconsciously taught to them in childhood.

Fourth Step

Now you're ready to underline the top three issues on the bad-side list that bug you the most, whether they're checked or not. You might use a different-colored pen to do so. Underline what triggers or upsets you the most in your life, not just from your partner or within yourself, but open it up to coming from anywhere such as friends, family, workmates, or even life in general.

Transfer those top three issues onto another sheet of paper or on the back of your worksheet. These are your top three active unhealed subconscious issues. These are the top three issues in your life that you wish you could heal enough so as to never have to deal with them again in your entire life, and if you did have to deal with them you'd know how, or it wouldn't even be an issue.

Top three active unhealed issues:

_____

Abandoning   Abusive   Bad Communicator

_____

Then go back to the sheet with your ten good and bad traits and see if there are any traits about your current or most recent partner that have surprised you that you never grew up with, that you weren't familiar with because they aren't in your ICOS/Template, and write them down outside the margin on each side, good and bad. As an example, maybe you grew up with adventurous not in your ICOS but have or had a partner who had that trait, and you loved it in them. That goes next to the good side and was a nice surprise for you, and it likely made up for some of the good traits you didn't check that keep you in the relationship more than if those extra traits weren't there.

Do the same on the bad side. An example here is maybe you grew up with parents who never cheated on each other, but your partner did, so that possibility wasn't even programmed into your nervous system (ICOS/Template). You could put cheater or betrayer in the margin outside the list of traits on the bad side because it was a trait that surprised you that you never grew up with and probably never even expected could happen. Or maybe needy or opportunistic or something else was a surprise bad trait. Just do as many as are true, and maybe there are none. Here's an example on the following page, including the three top traits you underlined earlier onto the bad side that still bug you the most:

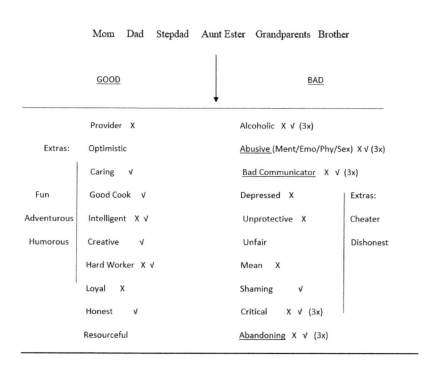

Mom   Dad   Stepdad   Aunt Ester   Grandparents   Brother

<u>GOOD</u>

<u>BAD</u>

	Provider X	Alcoholic X √ (3x)	
Extras:	Optimistic	<u>Abusive</u> (Ment/Emo/Phy/Sex) X√ (3x)	
	Caring √	<u>Bad Communicator</u> X √ (3x)	
Fun	Good Cook √	Depressed X	Extras:
Adventurous	Intelligent X √	Unprotective X	Cheater
Humorous	Creative √	Unfair	Dishonest
	Hard Worker X √	Mean X	
	Loyal X	Shaming √	
	Honest √	Critical X √ (3x)	
	Resourceful	<u>Abandoning</u> X √ (3x)	

X = 40% √ = 60%   X = 80% √ = 60%

Subconscious

With that, the "x-ray" is about half done. We've seen what traits you got programmed with growing up, both good and bad, that are the subconscious attractors that draw your "familiar" to you. Your subconscious isn't capable of judging these traits as good or bad, the traits are just what it must maintain - on a compulsory basis - because it's all it knows as its original programming. The good side doesn't need healing because it's already good and not problematic. It's only the bad traits or issues that give us angst and need healing, and we've narrowed it down to what your top three active unhealed subconscious issues are.

Here are the steps in brief:

1. Put the people who raised you and/or who influenced your childhood the most at the top of your page
2. List ten good traits and ten bad traits of all of them as if they were one person; they don't have to have any of the traits in common
3. Draw an arrow pointing down from the people who influenced you the most in childhood to the list of traits and write subconscious at the bottom of the page
4. Checkmark all the traits you see in your partner on both the good and bad side, and use Xs to mark any traits of an ex (if there was one)
5. Underline the top three issues that bother you the most in your life from anyone or anywhere whether they're already check marked or not
6. Transfer those top three issues to a new, blank circle.
7. In the margins of the lists of good and bad traits, write down any unfamiliar traits you did not grow up with that your partner has or had.

CHAPTER 2
THE DIAGNOSIS

Now that you know what you were programmed with by the people who influenced your childhood, which formed your ICOS - your Template and the neuropathways of your "Twelve" - and from there what your top three active unhealed subconscious issues are, we can move on to discovering your Core Wound. To do this, we must go back to how you felt overall as a child up to eleven years of age. The people who influenced our childhood the most did not give us our Core Wound intentionally; however, it was given to us as our programming, and we felt it without words, and we felt it deeply.

Our ICOS subconscious programming is complete before we are twelve, as we have experienced the separation of three umbilical cords: the physical, emotional, and mental. Obviously, our first umbilical cord is literally cut with our physical birth. The second is our emotional cord when we begin to realize we are not our mother's emotions and begin to separate from her emotionally, beginning at two years old. This takes until we're about seven, and then we become more interested in our father, as we begin to move from the emotional side of our being to more mental processes. (These are large, standard generalities). Before we're twelve the psychological "umbilical cord" is also cut when we realize we are independent from our father's thoughts, or anyone else's, and begin to think on our own. Our childhood is basically over at age twelve when we've gradually realized we are independent physically, emotionally and mentally from whatever mother and father figures we had. While still dependent upon them, in general, this marks the birth of our individual growth in those three combined ways and just in time for the arrival of puberty.

There are some rare exceptions, as when some extraordinary trauma has occurred enough to change a Core Wound after eleven years old. This could be the death of a parent or some major sexual abuse by a relative at age twelve or thirteen. I've even had clients (yes, plural) that have witnessed one of their parents during those years literally murder their spouse right in front of them. If something like that happens after thirteen, it's still possible but unlikely for a Core Wound to be changed. There are always exceptions but don't assume it. Our Core Wound is almost always branded in our brain for life by age eleven, and we actually have it much earlier, including a prenatal possibility.

Yes, a few clients received their Core Wound from their mother while they were in utero, so they were born with it and didn't realize it until they saw me. This will be understood later when we define what peptides are in Chapter 3; suffice it for now to know that a mother's emotional peptides can pass through the placenta and then attach to cell receptors within her unborn infant.

This is all said to prepare you for the Core Wound list: you want to *go back to how you felt as a child* and *feel* which of these statements feels most true. It's very unlikely that you put your Core Wound into words when you were that young, but you did feel it. You weren't rational as a child and your subconscious is also not rational, so *don't try to think and rationalize it yet.* You'll be able to put it all together and make sense of it later.

You don't need to know at this point which of these Core Wounds is the exact one, so I encourage you to just choose up to six. Ultimately, it will boil down to just one because it's the deepest *cause* of the others. The good news is you only have one Core Wound, and once you heal it, it is not replaced by another one. That one Core Wound will be the one that explains any of the others you chose to mark, as if all the issues in your Template and any of the other Core Wound possibilities are in a funnel, producing just one Core Wound that comes out of the funnel. Healing your Core Wound also heals everything in the funnel, the Template/ICOS.

You only have one Core Wound, and once you heal it, it is not replaced by another one.

Which of the following Core Wound statements "punches you in the gut" or "hurts your heart" the most? Which one feels the "heaviest?" Which one is the one you don't really want it to be even though you know it is? Which one intuitively stands out the most? Which one makes you feel "deeper underwater?" People often have an emotional reaction when they feel and recognize it. It's also a relief to know and to admit because now you know what to deal with, and now you know what has been subconsciously driving and/or undermining you all your life.

Another thing to be aware of, for those of you who think your Core Wound is "I will be abandoned," is to go deeper as to *why* you feel that or *why* you would be abandoned, and that *why* will lead you to a specific Core Wound. Your Core Wound is not a verb; it is an identity.

"I will be abandoned" is not a Core Wound.

Remember: feel it, don't think about it. We will double check it later to make certain it is correct because your one and only Core Wound is with you for life; however, once it's recognized and acknowledged (owned), you will learn how to neutralize it and forever deactivate its influence over you.

Go back to how you felt as a child and check up to six on the list below that you feel may be the one.

The Core Wound List:

✓ I am not good enough.
Something's wrong with me (and I don't know what it is).
I am not enough.
I never get it right.
I am not perfect enough.
I am not important.
I don't matter
I am flawed.
I am not worthy.
I am not valued.
I don't deserve.
Everyone else is more important than me.
I don't deserve love.
I am not acceptable the way I am.
I don't belong.
✓ I am not in charge of my own life.
✓ I am not safe.
✓ I am no one's priority.
I am not worthy of love.
I am not safe enough.
I am a problem.
I am a burden.
I am not wanted.
I am unlovable.
✓ I am on my own.
No one cares.

Now that you have checked up to six candidates as your Core Wound possibilities, we will do a process of elimination to get it down to one. It works best to still stay out of your rational brain to do so. If you've checked over six, you may be able to now whittle it down to six by realizing which ones are not the deepest truth. A lot of times it's just admitting the truth that you didn't know until you saw the phrase and felt it. Our Core Wound isn't usually something we want to admit even though we kind of already know it's the truth. It is, after all, our Core Wound, the inner world of our chronic, subconscious pain, so we've been trying to hide it from everyone, including ourselves, all our life. But when you're ready and willing to heal it, you'll finally want to see it so you can take it on and heal it to finally solve everything that doesn't work in your life. What a relief.

"Ahhh, my Core Wound is 'no one cares!' What a relief!" No, it's more like, "God, that's it! Bloody hell! I don't want to live with that reigning my life forever! I've got to heal this! It makes too much sense. Now I get it! I get why everything's been the way it is, and that my life's never going to work that way!"

Sometimes it's recognized with initial alarm. And also, don't over-rationalize it or try to psychoanalyze it or think you're the special exception to the rule because you can't figure it out. It's a knowing much deeper than your rational mind. It is an emotional, bodily felt, or intuitive knowing. Definitely do not let your Negative Ego figure it out for you; I've seen people do that, and it will get you nowhere. (Your Negative Ego will be thoroughly addressed elsewhere).

As you most likely have more than one phrase check marked, now we'll narrow it down to one. We'll do this by comparing two at a time with you still staying out of your rational brain.

Imagine you're wearing a sweatshirt or t-shirt that has the words of one of your Core Wound choices written on it, so people can read it. This shirt determines your self-image or self-esteem on *at least* a subliminal level. It is your IDENTITY. This shirt is a metaphor so you can feel how it feels to "wear the energy" of your Core Wound. How does it feel to wear the identity of "I don't matter," for example? What color shirt does "I don't matter" feel like? How does it feel on an emotional level or to imaginarily see yourself in a full-length mirror (at any age) wearing it, or walking around in public where people can read it? Or at home with your partner/spouse or around the kids. How heavy is it? Do you feel awkward, comfortable, or lousy wearing it? How does it fit? Is it new or old? **Especially, what emotions or feelings are attached to it? You must come up with three emotions** that being the person who is wearing "I don't matter" feels.

It's best to come up with the three emotions yourself, how each "shirt" feels, so I am intentionally not giving you a list of suggestions here, but some examples will be given later so you might hone in better if needed.

Now do the same thing with "I'm not good enough" (if that was one of your choices) and describe that metaphorical shirt. The key is the three emotions it makes you feel to become that person branded with that shirt. You will discover that none of the top three emotions that describe each "shirt" are of the same combination. So, comparing two at a time, which one feels most true? Especially which one hurts more? Which one feels like the one you don't really want people to see the most? Which one feels worse to wear or heavier emotionally? Which combination of emotions is your chronic pattern or where you habitually go to the most under stress? That's the one you choose, so you can scratch off the other Core Wound phrase.

Now choose two *other* Core Wounds and do the same thing until you've narrowed it down to three and then two. Or maybe you already know which one it is. If not, do the same process and compare the last two. Finally, if you still don't know – which is fine because you want to be certain – if you still don't know, then which one of the last two still remaining explains the other? "I don't matter" *because* "I'm not good enough," or, "I'm not good enough" *because* "I don't matter?" Rationally, you might think it's the first, but in my case (before I got to "no one cares") it was the latter. This is because it's an intuitive knowing more than a rational one, and because the subconscious mind does not think like the rational mind does; they're two different worlds. As an example, the dreams we have while sleeping come from our subconscious mind and usually don't even make sense to our conscious mind, at least without a lot of attention and interpretation, but it's just as real to itself as the conscious mind also is to itself.

After doing all this, you ought to have realized your one true Core Wound now. If not, you need to keep processing it until you get it before moving on to the next step.

Since this process didn't exist before, it took me longer to discover my Core Wound, and I lived with the "truth" that I was not good enough; I mean, that was obvious to me when I was in the throes of my healing. I never thought to review it for a long time; I just took the "truth" for granted. One day, when I was going through a bad phase, I got back into it, and I realized "I don't matter" was more true and deeper because it explained why I wasn't good enough: "I'm not good enough because I don't matter." It probably makes just as much sense the other way such as, "I don't matter because I'm not good enough," but for me the first example *felt* truer to me, so it also made more sense. This was the day I found my true Core Wound. I was so surprised that my deepest wound I had assumed for so long was, in fact, not the deepest truth that I asked myself if there was one that was even deeper than "I don't matter." This was before there was a list of Core Wounds, the rest of which have since come from clients. That's when "No one cares" hit me, and all the bells, whistles, and lights went on.

My brain suddenly lit up with awareness and memories and one-hundred percent certainty. I remembered feeling that way all the time as a kid, and I remembered singing the lyrics to myself of a song all the time in my teens and twenties with those exact words in it ("No one cares for me..."). It had even been my theme song! And I remembered experiences in my life I'd always had that proved it over and over. My brain went off like playing a pinball machine (ok, so I'm showing my age...) when you start winning a bunch of free games, as it starts making all kinds of noise and clicking loudly each time you've reached another threshold of points; there's extra balls zipping around and you get to flip the flippers like mad, racking up the points like crazy, all kinds of colors are flashing, your heart's beating harder, and the dopamine's going off in your head.

Or some people just sob.

But I'd done enough of all that all my life in my depression and self-pity (self-pity being absolutely worthless in retrospect), so I loved my brain going off when I discovered my true Core Wound, though it was a whole-body experience, too.

It was also the beginning of my ultimate healing.

Realizing your Core Wound is the beginning of your ultimate healing.

Now don't worry, you don't have to have a lit-up brain or wet yourself to know your Core Wound, but some people do; nonetheless, it is always a big aha moment that begins to explain everything. Your own process has its own timing and its own intensity; our processes are all different.

***

Now we'll re-visit your "x-ray" sheet, the one with those who influenced your childhood the most and their good and bad traits, your Template. First, on that sheet, write down your Core Wound somewhere in the space at the top of the page. Let's say it's "I am not wanted." (The quote marks indicate "supposedly"). Write it like this:

Core Wound:

"I am not wanted."

Now, underneath that, in red ink, write: IT'S A LIE!

For the first time in your life, you've discovered your Core Wound, and your subconscious is now on notice that it's a lie. Every Core Wound is a lie. You may not believe it's a lie yet, but the seed is now planted in your conscious and subconscious.

Your Core Wound was given to you, and it developed in you by the way you subjectively interpreted your childhood experiences. It also determines what triggers you, what your issues are, and what influences your "Twelve." It has been an emotional and psychological habit that's been with you all your life. Neuropathways in your brain have been strongly developed like superhighways, and cell receptors have increased throughout your brain, heart, and gut that starve for the emotional peptides, literally as an addiction to those emotions that your Core Wound creates. It has been the comfort zone and normal you were programmed with since childhood, and it gets activated especially when you're under stress or worn out. It even causes a lot of your stress through your "Twelve." Your Core Wound is the base from where all your negative thoughts, unhealthy emotions, and unhealthy behavior come from.

Your Core Wound is the base from where all your negative thoughts, unhealthy emotions, and unhealthy behavior come from.

We have already extracted what your top three active unhealed issues are. Now write your Core Wound in the same area you created where you wrote those top three active unhealed subconscious issues in. You'll now have four statements in there, but your Core Wound is the cause of the other three you first wrote down. Originally, the traits – what became the issues you were programmed with - caused your Core Wound, but now your Core Wound maintains your issues; they support one another back and forth like a positive feedback loop (positive feedback loops feed and sustain one another, and the positive is similar to a medical diagnosis being bad news). Your Core Wound has been underneath your conscious awareness until now, but it has been the basis of your subconscious reality creation.

Using another metaphor, your Core Wound is like a mushroom "plant" (for the record, a mushroom is not a plant but rather a fungus), and your issues are like the mushrooms that pop up from it. A mushroom is not the mushroom "plant." The "plant" grows under the surface (it is the white fibrous stuff called mycelium); this is like our Core Wound, which is under the surface of our conscious mind. Like fruit, mushrooms are only the reproductive part of the "plant" that spring up in various places like your issues do from your Core Wound. The point is, your top three issues are directly connected to your Core Wound like mushrooms are connected to the large, underground "plant."

As it makes sense to you, draw an arrow from your Core Wound to each of your top three issues. Previously, we have already identified them in our example as abusive, bad communicator, and abandoning. This means you would be triggered the most into feeling/thinking you are not wanted from being abused, badly communicated to, and/or abandoned. These top three issues are the most direct hits that activate your Core Wound. These three are like the dive-bomber airplanes that went straight down towards the enemy aircraft carriers in WWII to hit their target.

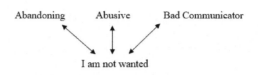

Top three active unhealed issues:

Abandoning   Abusive   Bad Communicator

I am not wanted

Now go to the "x-ray" sheet with all the other bad traits listed that you grew up with, and the other unfamiliar traits you added in the margin of the bad list, and underline all the issues you now can see or realize come from your Core Wound. It's probably most of them if you really think about it, but maybe not quite as acutely as your top three. Then write somewhere on that page, "Underlined = all the issues that trigger my Core Wound."

Your Core Wound is like a spider in a web (your ICOS/Template), and every time a bug (an issue/trait) hits the web, the spider reacts to it.

The next step is to use a symbol (a triangle used here) to mark all the traits you grew up with on the bad side that are *your reactive behavior* when you're triggered. Afterall, the ones that influenced your childhood the most taught you how to react by their own examples. In the margin, you might come up with some extras you do on your own that you didn't grow up with. Then write, "Δ = my reactive behavior when my Core Wound is triggered."

The following page is an example of how a completed "x-ray" could look.

Core Wound: "I am not wanted"

IT'S A LIE!

	Mom	Dad	Stepdad	Aunt Ester	Grandparents	Brother

GOOD   ↓   BAD

	GOOD		BAD	
	Provider X		Alcoholic X √ (3x)	
	Optimistic		Δ Abusive (Ment/Emo/Phy/Sex) X √ (3x)	
Extras:	Caring √		Δ Bad Communicator X √ (3x)	
Fun	Good Cook √		Δ Depressed X	Extras:
Adventurous	Intelligent X √		Unprotective X	Cheater
Humor	Creative √		Unfair	Liar
	Hard Worker X √		Mean X	
	Loyal X		Shaming √	
	Honest √		Δ Critical X √ (3x)	Δ Isolate
	Resourceful		Δ Abandoning X √ (3x)	

X = 40% √ = 60%   X = 80% √ = 60%

Underlined = all the issues that trigger my Core Wound (12)

Δ = my reactive behavior (6)
(I cannot blame this on anyone else!)

Subconscious

At this point, 1) you are now conscious of how you were programmed as a child; 2) you are now conscious of the result, your Core Wound; 3) you are now conscious of what triggers your Core Wound; and 4) you are now conscious of what your reactive behavior is when your Core Wound is activated. To heal anything only requires consciousness and willpower, and now you have four levels of consciousness about your Core Wound. You will soon be using Consciousness and Willpower to heal your Core Wound ("...use C&W to heal your CW").

Diagnosis steps in brief:

1. Go back to how you felt as a child and checkmark up to six Core Wounds that best describe how you felt.
2. "Wear" a shirt with one Core Wound written on it to see how it feels to you emotionally when you put it on. Describe it with three emotions. Do the same thing with another Core Wound to "wear," and then compare the two to feel which one is truer and hurts more and/or which emotions have been more chronic for you, so you can eliminate the lesser Core Wound one at a time.
3. When you get it down to two, feel, intuit, realize and/or admit which one feels worse (like step 2) and explains the other or is the cause of the other.
4. Write down your Core Wound, put it in quotes, and write "IT'S A LIE!" in red underneath it.
5. Transfer your Core Wound to the area with your three top issues in it and recognize (with arrows) how they are directly connected to your Core Wound.
6. Underline any of the other traits on the bad side (the x-ray sheet) that you now can see are connected to your Core Wound (what triggers you), even if indirectly.

7. Use a symbol (a triangle used as example) to mark any bad traits you grew up with in the "x-ray" from your main influencers that describes your reactive behavior when you're triggered, and add any others in the margin that you came up with yourself.

Once you've done these steps, you can realize and be conscious of how you operate. On your worksheet, you should now have most of the bad traits underlined, which is to show you which issues trigger you into your Core Wound. And you'll now have a symbol to show you what your reactive behavior is when you're triggered. You may have already added some other triggers outside the circle that were a surprise that you didn't grow up with from some relationship you had or have that are underlined (such as cheater, for example). There may also be some reactive behaviors of yours you could add that are specific to your own adaptation that you didn't grow up with that are marked with a symbol (maybe you isolate, for example).

You want to be especially cognizant of your own reactive behavior. You cannot blame anyone else for your own reactive behavior even if someone else triggered you. Then you can trace it back to which specific issue triggered your Core Wound in whatever situation did so. Then you can consciously do something about it called healing!

You cannot blame anyone else for your own reactive behavior even though someone else triggered you.

You can consciously override the ICOS/Template with conscious choice. You can talk to your partner (or, if appropriate or conducive, whoever else may have triggered your Core Wound), to help resolve the issue and heal. This would go something like, "When you criticize me I react in anger because I feel not wanted. My reactive anger is something I don't like any more than you do, and I'm working on consciously not reacting this way. But it would also greatly help if you were conscious enough not to trigger me in the first place by not criticizing me like you do." That's what healthy people do who love one another: communicate, and consciously and willingly change their behavior for the sake of cultivating their love for one another.

Here's an example from my own life of how this works. It's easy to think one has healed all their issues when one is not in an intimate relationship because there's no one there to trigger, challenge, or mirror our issues back to us so intensely. As this Core Wound system developed over time, I had identified twenty-six issues/traits on the bad side that my ICOS was programmed with, and as I continued to heal, none of them had been triggered in a long time. But once I had gotten into a new relationship, I eventually got triggered. My reactive behavior was anger, which I didn't like any more than my partner did, and it was a surprise to both of us. As soon as I had the chance, I found my x-ray sheet and reviewed those twenty-six traits; one was "dismissive." Being dismissed triggered "No one cares," my Core Wound, which was then followed by my reactive behavior. By pinpointing the exact issue (I'd forgotten it was even there), I was able to talk to my partner about it, and we both got it. I didn't want to act that way once I got triggered, so I'm the one that had to be proactive about it, and she didn't want to trigger me by unknowingly dismissing me and then also reacting to my anger with her anger. Only a couple of more less-triggering instances came up that caught us off guard, but that was enough for us to catch on and heal that dynamic!

It's amazing how miniscule some things can trigger such big reactions, but the more specific we get, the deeper the healing is. "Love pays attention to detail" is a statement I have found to be very true, and it's not that hard, not that complicated, and not that time-consuming at all to get to the details. The opposite of love is apathy (not hate, anger, or fear), so paying attention to detail shows you care and makes your loved one feel loved.

Consciousness of your own issues, the willingness to heal, and healthy communication with someone of similar consciousness and willingness is the key to a healthy relationship, as is paying attention to detail and acting upon it. Again, it all boils down to healing your own Core Wound and being conscious of what your loved ones' Core Wounds are. The commitment to healing our own Core Wound first makes us able and willing to do so.

The opposite of love is apathy. Love pays attention to detail.

It would be a very good idea to write down and memorize the list of all the traits that trigger your partner's Core Wound so you're conscious of how *not* to trigger them anymore. This is also great so you can protect or support your partner when other people trigger them.

As a couple, you want to memorize your partner's list of traits that trigger them, so you become conscious of how <u>not</u> to trigger them anymore.

I have jumped ahead a bit with this example… there is more to go about how to heal your Core Wound. Next is getting to know the Negative Ego and how it works and what it does to you.

CHAPTER 3
THE NEGATIVE EGO

"Until you make the unconscious conscious, it will direct your life, and you will call it fate." Carl Jung

Again, the "Twelve" represent the synergistic <u>resonance</u> of your thoughts, feelings, attitudes, choices, beliefs, desire, imagination, expectation, behavior, perspective, dreams, and will. Healing your Core Wound will change all of these.

Of course, we've all heard of the ego. Our ego is simply our self-image, which also is our self-esteem. It is necessary in order to give us a sense of self, of individuality, an I. As a metaphor, the ego is like the membrane of a cell, separating the rest of the cell from its external world, or as a human is like an individual cell in the body of humanity. The "membrane" is what allows the various experiences and influences of life to pass in and out of the cell, the self.

The job of a properly functioning ego is simply to deliver information, to objectively pass it through the "membrane" from the external world to our internal world, and vice versa, like a post office person delivers mail. Our ego is supposed to just be the messenger for our self; it was never meant to even read the mail let alone interpret what it means. This is key to understand, as our interpretation of the outer world determines our inner sense of self, our placement of self in the world.

The problem is, we have defaulted to our subconscious to remain in charge of our ego's delivery system, which functions out of our ICOS programming – the neuropathways developed in and still existing from our childhood - and our ICOS is founded upon our Core Wound. In turn, since our Negative Ego is fully based upon our Core Wound, it is the voice of our Core Wound, and it very subjectively interprets reality for us through its negative lens, the "membrane." Our Negative Ego sees through the lens of our Core Wound. Thus, as we remain unaware of our Core Wound/Lie and our Negative Ego/Liar, we also automatically react out of the ICOS.

Our Negative Ego is the subconscious voice of our Core Wound; it is the way our subconscious expresses our Core Wound.

Our Negative Ego has reign over our "Twelve" because it started when we were so young and vulnerable. The "Twelve" has thus become so normal that we've never even questioned what our Negative Ego has kept saying to us. The "Twelve" becomes our self-image/self-esteem, or how we see or place ourselves in our environment from our Negative Ego's interpretation both from the inside out and from the outside in.

Our Negative Ego is not that smart; it just keeps saying the same things about us and others and life in general over and over, yet we believe it every time. Our Negative Ego has an easy but very boring job, but as we continually fall for its version of reality, it has zero respect for us. It's like a tape recorder that bubbles up from our subconscious: just "push one of our buttons" and off it goes, triggered by our issues (all those traits in the "x-ray" on the bad side that got programmed into us), and our reactive thoughts, emotions, and behavior kick into gear. This behavior, in turn, ends up creating the same results we've always had that "proves" our Core Wound, and our Negative Ego gets to be "right."

Remember, our subconscious can only recreate what it knows, over and over, as its job is to maintain the status quo, and it does so exclusively, continually, and automatically. Our subconscious is incapable of varying outside of its programming.

Our Negative Ego's voice is always a very unloving voice that perpetrates mental and emotional abuse upon us. The Negative Ego is not our friend, and we do not need to be nice to it whatsoever; it is actually our worst enemy. And in case you think you can love your Negative Ego into being healed, know this: your Negative Ego will *never* love you back.

Your Negative Ego will *never* love you.

The part of us that is the source of all our negativity, in all its forms, and all of our self-deprecation and self-sabotage is our Negative Ego. It determines - and undermines - our self-esteem. All of the various Core Wounds undermine our self-esteem each to their own degree, and some are more shame-based than others.

As long as we allow our Negative Ego to create our reality according to the Core Wound we've been branded with, we are severely compromised and limited by our "Twelve." This makes us Masters of Limitation because of our comfort zone, our "familiar." Until we become consciously aware of our Negative Ego's *ad nauseum* interpretations of reality, our "Twelve" will be heavily tinted by our Negative Ego. It is the part of us that needs healing - like putting the worst kind of criminal away for life helps heal society.

We are prisoners of our Negative Ego until we put our Negative Ego in prison.

Once we become consciously aware of our Negative Ego's reactive "Twelve," it then becomes a conscious choice and/or lack of willpower to continue to be governed by its voice. Instead, we need as much ammo as possible against our Negative Ego/Liar, and this ammo comes in the form of consciously telling the truth about ourselves no matter how great or small that truth is.

Once we see what we are telling ourselves through our Negative Ego, we will easily recognize that *in no way* is it the voice of self-love.

After you're conscious of what it says, there's no reason to ever again listen to your Negative Ego! You just have to get really good at breaking the habit. You will then know better than to waste any more time wallowing around with your Core Wound/Lie and your Negative Ego/Liar.

As long as we are allowing our Core Wound to be the "truth," we are allowing the "Twelve" of our ICOS to determine what our "Twelve" are as an adult. We may have adapted our Inner Child's programming to fit into the adult world, but the Core Wound - the foundation and root cause of the dysfunctional part of our inner world - remains the same. This gives us a profound bias as to how we personally see the world.

Our Negative Ego interprets reality for us through the lens of our Core Wound as long as we let it.

Like cherry-picking reality to prove what it "knows" is wrong with us, our Negative Ego selectively interprets reality to confirm our Core Wound programming. This function is known as confirmation bias. Regarding the Core Wound, confirmation bias is the tendency for people to subconsciously select information that already confirms their "Twelve." People also tend to *reject* evidence that contradicts their "Twelve." This selectivity by our Negative Ego prevents our ability to receive or recognize anything contrary to the Lie, so the truth remains unbelievable and un-receivable.

Another function of confirmation bias is in recalling memories that only reinforce our Core Wound's story, a subconscious story usually of pain and definitely of limitation and self-sabotage. Such chronically recalled memories are referred to as anchors. Psychological anchors keep us stuck in place, more or less, within a spectrum of trauma from events in our lives we focus on that define and support our self-image born of pain. These anchors are very often accompanied with PTSD (Post-Traumatic Stress Disorder).

Overall, it is very common as adults to be completely brainwashed by our Negative Ego.

Nothing changes until we consciously change it, and we have to correctly identify what to change in order to heal it properly.

You either consciously heal your Core Wound, or you end up continually recreating it subconsciously throughout your life.

Up to now, our subconscious has held most of the power of our overall consciousness. Our subconscious is vast and remembers everything we've ever experienced; it is essentially infinite compared to our conscious awareness. (What did you get for Christmas when you were eleven? What was the license plate number of that car that backed into you twelve years ago? Your subconscious knows.) Compared to our subconscious our conscious awareness is miniscule, yet is has the power to overrule our subconscious because our conscious mind has the power of choice. The subconscious does not have the capacity to make a conscious choice; that's why it's called *sub*conscious. The seat of our power is in our conscious mind. As a metaphor, it's like a king's ability to override an entire country and even its history. It is because our conscious mind has the power of choice that our conscious mind has more power than our vast subconscious - but we have to use it!

"The seat of our power is in our conscious mind."[4]

The same things may be going on in the world, but by healing our Core Wound we can interpret and experience them in an entirely different and more objective way. Our experiences even change, as we heal our shame and raise our self-image up out of our previous Core Wound muck and mire. We get to choose - and even amplify that choice with conscious commitment. Imagine how much can change when we consciously heal our internal Lie and its voice of the Liar rather than to continually react because of it!

With willpower, we can change the "c" ("c" = consciousness) from "c" being in the midst of reaCtion to "c" being at the beginning of Creation.[5] Reaction or creation, the same alignment of the same letters, just move the "c," our consciousness, to start consciously creating rather than leaving our consciousness in the middle of subconsciously reacting. Consciously creating our inner world also changes the reflections of, or feedback from, our outer world and what we attract from it. It also ends the unfulfilling drama or dysfunction of our reactive behavior.

Change the "c" in reaCtion (subcon.) to the beginning of Creation (conscious).

When our Negative Ego is finally realized consciously and put in its place, all the reactionary behavior that comes from our "issues" ("triggers") are finally put to rest because all of our issues come from our Core Wound. Yes, we can actually live our lives without being triggered all the time instead of reacting from our Negative Ego.

Our thoughts and emotions are not separate; thoughts create emotions, and emotions create thoughts. They form a positive feedback loop always in support of each other. However, when we become conscious of *why* we feel the way we do, it is then we are able to make a conscious choice of how to respond rather than let the subjective Negative Ego go wild within and react. Because thoughts and feelings feed each other, the same is equally true when we become conscious of when our Negative Ego is doing our thinking. When we heal our Core Wound, we are able to stop subconsciously reacting because we know why we have the issues we have. As we stay committed to maintaining our consciousness and willpower to heal our Core Wound, all our issues begin to evaporate as well as our reactive behavior caused by them. We are then able to consciously choose to replace self-sabotage and limitation with any kind of inner and outer qualities we want to be or be with.

To catch your Negative Ego in the act of lying, it helps greatly to remember the primary emotions of your Core Wound, the ones you identified when you discovered it in the previous chapter. How does your Core Wound make you feel? Once you recognize you are in the normal, comfort-zone feelings of your Core Wound – such as anger, depression, anxiety, etc. - you can then become aware of what is being voiced by your Negative Ego, for it is the voice of those reactive emotions stemming from your Core Wound. It is in that moment you can learn to stop the Liar and the reactive "Twelve"; otherwise, that "moment" can last all day or all year into decades. It is in those moments when you catch your Negative Ego lying that you can stop your reactive self-sabotage and literally cause neuroplasticity: consciously creating new neuropathways!

To heal our Core Wound we must get to the point of catching our Negative Ego lying *in the moment* and correct it in the moment with conscious truth.

Our Core Wound is comprised of only about three primary emotions, which we have literally become addicted to. The emotions of our Core Wound feel very normal no matter what they are; they are our "favorite worst feelings." We actually become physically addicted to the emotions of our Core Wound through the peptides these emotions create, especially since they've been with us since childhood.

Peptides are chemicals in our bloodstream such as oxytocin, adrenalin, estrogen, testosterone, and hundreds more. (Before a *bio-electric* communication system was developed in lifeforms - what we call a nervous system - all life had a *bio-chemical* communication system, which functions with peptides rather than nerve cells. As humans, we have both systems, the peptide system being primordial.) Some peptides are called *The Molecules of Emotion*[6] (Candace Pert, another extraordinary genius, scientist, author pioneer), so every emotion we feel creates a specific peptide.

Since childhood, the cells of our body, especially in our brain and according to our ICOS/Template, have had cell receptors for these peptides for emotions such as depression, shame, anxiety, etc., and these receptors crave to be continuously filled. These starving cell receptors also increase in number the more they get fed and are positioned all along our ICOS neuropathways. This is why as long as we allow our Negative Ego to lie and dictate our "Twelve," we will be functioning from our "familiar," and literally addicted to our subconscious reactiveness, even being defensive of it, and always feeling basically the same way we always have. This also explains our recurring patterns of self-sabotage and self-fulfilling prophecy. We become addicted to our story of pain, subconsciously recreating it over and over, all fed with lies, and all based on our Core Wound.

We become emotionally peptide-addicted to our story of pain, subconsciously recreating it over and over, all fed with lies.

The Negative Ego's voice is like the lyrics of a song that are stuck in our head, a song which makes us feel the emotions we've become addicted to from our Core Wound. Our Negative Ego/Liar's message profoundly and actively impacts our lives. The key is to become conscious of what our Negative Ego is saying and have the willpower to truly heal it.

***

In preparation for the following worksheet, you will use the three emotional words you came up with to describe how the Core Wound "shirt" you decided on made you feel when you were "wearing" it. Not everyone is great at identifying emotions, which is fine, so I help them all the time. The following list is only here to help you hone in more if you find that there are some more accurate emotions connected to your Core Wound than you were able to identify before. But *please* don't just pick carelessly or mentally from the list; *you need to feel them*: lonely, depressed, alienated, embarrassed, sad, hopeless, helpless, angry, fearful, anxious, despair, melancholy, scared, sorrow, empty, overwhelmed, unsafe, bereft, disdain, cautious, mortified, distress, apologetic, shame, forlorn, defeated, dejected, discouraged, disappointed, longing, envy, jealous, resentful, hurt, unworthy, pathetic, and confused. I'm certain there are many more.

Many people use verbs to describe how they feel such as, "I feel abandoned." But verbs are not emotions; they are actions. Since verbs are actions, getting to an emotion is about how we feel about those actions. How do you feel about being abandoned or any other verbs that happened to you? Two other words people identify with their Core Wound – guilt or numb - are also not emotions. So for numb, guilt, and verbs – especially abandoned - go deeper to feel what emotions are underneath those.

For instance, ponder this: Guilt is anger we don't feel we have a right to have.

Guilt is anger we don't feel we have a right to have.

It's better to admit what the anger's about and feel it rather than just feeling guilt because guilt is "no movement." (I advise some clients to make a list of what they are angry about but never feel or admit because they feel guilt instead). Guilt will keep you stuck forever until you admit and feel the emotion guilt is covering up. A classic example would be, maybe you're really angry about your mother, but "it's not ok" to feel that way about her, so you feel guilty about it and instead bury the anger with guilt.

When I healed my anger instead of burying it with guilt, my relationships no longer necessitated reflecting back my denied anger. Beforehand, my anger had come out in me in reactive and misdirected ways. Once I had gotten to the cause of my anger and the emotional reality of it by feeling and safely expressing it with no guilt, this greatly helped me in no longer being subconsciously attracted to angry, misandrist women that subconsciously reminded me of my mother who was a great source of my Wound. (Misandrists are generally women who hate men although men can be misandrists, too, just as women can also be misogynists).

The other preparation for the following worksheet is that, to expose your Negative Ego and its lies, you need to write them in second-person, using "you" or "you are" rather than "I" or "me." This is so it will be as if your Negative Ego is talking *to* you outside of yourself. Here's an example: "*You* will never be successful" rather than, "I will never be successful"; or, "No one will ever understand *you*" rather than, "No one will ever understand me." This is personifying your Negative Ego to extract it out from you, so you can see it for what it is rather than *being* it so much as you have.

As a reminder back from the beginnings of Chapter 1:

Our Core Wound is not a core belief. It is deeper. Our Core Wound is our Identity. Our Identity is the foundational cause of our limiting beliefs. Our limiting beliefs effortlessly maintain our subconscious Identity and thus our personal inner and outer reality.

Worksheet

Core Wound: " _I am unsafe_ ."

Since your Core Wound is the Lie, your Negative Ego is the Liar. Your Negative Ego (negative self-image) is the subconscious voice of your Core Wound. _Every time you are feeling the primary emotions of your Core Wound, your Negative Ego is subconsciously telling you the lies of your Core Wound._

List the primary emotions of your core wound:

~~fearful~~   so Vunerable ~~unsafe~~   lonely

This is what determines your inner and outer reactive thoughts, feelings, behavior, beliefs and much more (the "Twelve") until you consciously choose otherwise. You must know what your Negative Ego says to you in order to become conscious enough of it to choose otherwise and deactivate your Negative Ego's influence. List what it tells you here (you already know it by heart) and write these subconscious lies in second-person ("you" statements, not "I" or "me" statements) and in black ink. Leave room to write something else in between the lines later.

1. ~~You~~ are not loveable
2. You are ignored
3. You are not appreciated
4. You are neglected
5. You are no-one's priority
6. You are not wanted
7.

72

This starts the process of catching the lies. List at least twenty more lies now; the more the better in order to become conscious of your Negative Ego's lies. Do this for as long as it takes. Do it until you're so aware of them that you don't even have to write them down. It has been a life-long bad habit, an emotional addiction, and your "comfort zone."

Worksheet, Example 1

Core Wound: "_____I am not wanted._____."

Since your Core Wound is the Lie, your Negative Ego is the Liar. Your Negative Ego (negative self-image) is the subconscious voice of your Core Wound. *Every time* you are feeling the primary emotions of your Core Wound, your Negative Ego is subconsciously telling you the lies of your Core Wound.

List the primary emotions of your core wound:

_____Sad_____   _____Anxious_____   _____Insecure_____

This is what determines your inner and outer reactive thoughts, feelings, behavior, beliefs and much more (the "Twelve") until you consciously choose otherwise. You must know what your Negative Ego says to you in order to become conscious enough of it to choose otherwise and deactivate your Negative Ego's influence. List what it tells you here (you already know it by heart) and write these subconscious lies in second-person ("you" statements, not "I" or "me" statements) and in black ink. Leave room to write something else in between the lines later.

1. You're stupid.
2. You'll never have any friends.
3. You'll never be successful.
4. You'll never fit in.
5. People will always take advantage of you.
6. You're better off alone.
7. You're such a phony.

This starts the process of catching the lies, which are also your limiting *beliefs* that spring from your Core Wound. List at least twenty more lies now; the more the better in order to become conscious of your Negative Ego's lies. Do this for as long as it takes. Do it until you're so aware of them that you don't even have to write them down and can bust them in real-time. It is a life-long bad habit, an emotional addiction, and your "comfort zone."

MEET YOUR INNER CHILD

The Inner Child is much more than just a concept, and the importance of meeting and healing your Inner Child is an essential part to healing your Core Wound. This is because your Core Wound developed in your childhood, which became your operating system, your ICOS. Your Core Wound is how your subconscious runs your negative self-image, so healing your Inner Child is a huge part of healing your Core Wound. The voice of your Core Wound begins with the pain of your Inner Child.

Our unhealed inner and outer reactions are due to the programming we had in our childhood.

I have found that we aren't truly in our adult or grown-up self until we heal our Core Wound; this is because we are still dominated by and reacting out of our Inner Child's pain or mindset in very subtle or not so subtle ways, triggered most of the time.

After having written at least seven of the lies your Negative Ego tells you, now you need to realize the impact of what you have been doing to yourself all your life since childhood. It is crucial to realize and acknowledge the impact we have on our own Inner Child in order to love our Inner Child into being healed.

We *are* the Future Self of our Inner Child; that is not a theory. And with an unhealed Core Wound, we are still telling our own Inner Child the same things he or she were feeling in childhood. We, as our Inner Child's Future Self, have kept alive the same indoctrination or ICOS that we grew up with as a kid, but now we are doing it to ourselves with nobody else to blame. We do this because we are unaware of our subconscious programming having become so normal since we were children, firing away on the freeways of our neuropathways that formed way back then.

No matter our age, we've been triggered by our same Core Wound ever since childhood and then, until healed, have taken our reactivity out on ourselves and those we love (self-sabotage).

You may or may not have ever heard of the concept of us all having an Inner Child, but he or she is actual and very real. Your Inner Child is real, and he/she never died. Every full-grown tree was a little sapling to begin with, but that sapling never died; it became the trunk that holds up the entire adult tree, very alive and well, and the five-year-old tree rings are still there to prove it. Metaphorically, the sapling is our Inner Child, programmed with the ICOS, and the psychological/emotional composition of the ICOS is still very much alive within us as adults, just like the tree rings, as long as we have not healed our Core Wound.

Our Core Wound began when we were children and, left unhealed, continues on into our adulthood. Therefore, our Inner Child is the foundation of our "Twelve" and all of our reactive behavior. As adults, we have learned to adapt our Inner Child to the adult world, so it's not like we are outwardly acting as children in the world, but our inner world is still based off the unhealed ICOS. Without making conscious choices to override our ICOS, our subconscious programming is still running our lives psychologically, emotionally, and behaviorally. The Wound within our ICOS is our most basic law of attraction within our subconscious and why the same patterns keep showing up in our lives.

In order to realize the effect we have upon ourselves as the Future Self of our own Inner Child, it's mandatory to tell him or her about our Core Wound. No one can give you willpower, but this next, required, short little technique ought to give you a reason to have it. The Core Wound, the Negative Ego, and the primary emotions of your Core Wound are all the same thing; they all sustain one another as a whole. They are you your "normal," your Template/ICOS that has been with you for life.

Sit down and relax. Imagine your Inner Child standing in front of you so you are eye-level with one another. Picture them as vividly as you can, such as what type and color of clothing they're wearing and their hairstyle, etc. Most of all, notice what the expression on their face is as they are looking right into your eyes, their Future Self, the one they depend on the most. Take your glasses off so they can see your eyes. Make it real.

Now tell them your Core Wound, and say it in "you" form instead of "I" form, whichever Core Wound you/they have. For instance, if your Core Wound is, "I am not wanted," tell your Inner Child, "Hi (name or nickname they had as a child), I'm your Future Self, and I'm here to tell you that... you are not wanted." Their own Future Self is telling them they are not wanted! (Which *is* what you have been showing and saying to them all these years.) Go on and tell them the rest of it. Do it. I know you probably don't want to, but you must realize your impact, and you only have to do this once in your life if you do it for real. Be present. Don't just rush through it, *feel* it, and *do it:*

> "You are stupid.
>
> You'll never have any friends.
>
> You'll never be successful.
>
> You'll never fit in.
>
> People will always take advantage of you.
>
> You are better off alone.
>
> You're a phony!"

How does that make your Inner Child feel, and what's the expression on their face now? This is what you, through your Negative Ego, have been telling them/you all your life and what you are doing to yourself as long as you do not heal your Core Wound.

Pretty impactful, isn't it. A lot of my clients are already crying before they do it and normally are crying hard by the time they're done. As it should be. Make it real when you do it. Your Inner Child is real.

Your inner child is real

Some people "can't" do it, but I strongly suggest you do. If you're truly present for this and do it for real, you only need to ever do it once. *Now you know the impact of what you've been doing to your own Inner Child/yourself all your life by not healing your Core Wound.* To do this is to give yourself the most impactful reason to have the willpower you need to heal. You would never say to your own kids (or anyone else's) whatever Negative Ego lies you just said to your own Inner Child. But you actually *do* say them to your own Inner Child every time you think or feel them because he or she is in there! *And you are the only one doing it!!* (Unless you have created a partner that has become your own Negative Ego personified, telling you things similar as to what you just said to your own Inner Child). You must know by now that doing so must end, starting as of this moment, doing the best you can until you've reprogrammed yourself enough to create your life with conscious truth rather than subconscious lies.

You create an entirely different reality when you create your life with conscious truth rather than subconscious lies.

Not to leave you with feeling the impact you're having on your own Inner Child. now, when you're ready, you can avow to commit to healing your Inner Child. Tell them right now, as they still stand in front of you, with full feeling, maybe with tears still spread all over your face, with full commitment: "I commit to healing us! I commit to healing our Core Wound! I commit to healing you. I commit to protecting you from our Negative Ego!" Now how do they feel? You are literally the only one that can heal your own Inner Child.

Please take the time and create the space to both read the Lies to your Inner Child in order to realize the impact and pain you are keeping alive and to commit to healing your Core Wound for them (together) with an Authentic Rite of Passage, so it really means something. *This needs to be <u>much more</u> than just mental or just reading about it.*

You are the only one that can heal your own Inner Child.

As the Future Self of our own Inner Child, we must be the protector of that little girl or little boy. With healthy boundaries, we must be the filter that does not allow any form of abuse or shame or wounding to ever happen to them again, especially from our own Negative Ego. Doing this for our Inner Child will also heal our life as their Future Self. Although we cannot say we are our Inner Child's parent, we can be their Conscious Parent/Future Self that "re-parents" them. We must be the one that restores them and perhaps becomes the first one to ever give them the comfort, love, compassion, understanding, or anything else they've always wanted or needed. Your Inner Child grew up with that wound. It's *your job* to make sure your Inner Child is correctly taken care of *by you*. Would you shame your own Inner Child? Are *you* now the one that's never there for them like it was for them in childhood? Would you allow or do *any* of those bad traits you grew up with to be done to them by *you* or anyone else? And he or she is just *dying* in there hearing it from their own Future Self! And you wonder why you feel lousy all day?

My Inner Child was thinking of suicide all throughout his childhood, but now he and his Future Self (me) exchange joy to each other all the time. He loves me and trusts me wholly, feels totally safe, and is still amazed that I succeeded so much in actually healing us. He thinks I'm his superhero and is forever in awe, totally secure to be who he is, to dream his dreams, and feel unconditionally loved. I love him to tears; he was smart enough and tough enough to survive our childhood and save his Future Self's life. Healing him got me to the platform of joy and unconditional love for the rest of my/our life. Most of all, we're free of our story of pain and the addiction to it that defined us and our "Twelve" with all its old resonance and patterns and attractions. We're free to be healed, and instead of being forever wounded we have an entirely new destiny.

Healing your Inner Child is the greatest act of self-love you can give yourself.

So, back to your commitment... you better mean it; your Inner Child's counting on you now. Once you become aware of a pattern that doesn't work, it then becomes a choice you are making if you continue to do it. Plus you made a commitment to them. Let them help you; they'd love to. Allow your Inner Child to remind you, for instance, and tell you, their Future Self, "That doesn't work anymore, remember?"

Be their superhero for them. You can find joy by healing your Inner Child because all your pain began with them and your ICOS.

***

Now we're going to go back to our present worksheet. On the back of it or on a new page, title the page with the opposite of your Core Wound. For example, if your Core Wound is "I don't matter," you would write, "How I matter." If it's "I'm not good enough," write, "How I am good enough." Do this with whatever Core Wound you have. ("Something's wrong with me [and I don't know what it is]" is the only CW that needs two columns; one is headed with "What's right with me" and the other column is, "What I know I need to heal.") Then make as long of a list as you can that tells you the truth. These can be general statements or just one word or so. Usually, it's something like, "I am sensitive; I am compassionate; I am generous; I am a good mother; I own a successful business…". Hopefully, the list goes on and on.

If you get stuck at this, as many people do, it will help to bring your Inner Child in again and tell him or her, as their Future Self, how their life is going to turn out on the positive side. Something like, "Honey, I know you feel like something's wrong with you (and you don't know what it is) – we both have up until this point – but you're going to turn out to be a multimillionaire at only twenty-nine years of age! So I must have done something right! Now I can see that I loved and trusted my sisters enough to go into business with them because we're all so bonded, intelligent, motivated and capable! I'm really good at phone and computer technology and even set up our business' global website! I now see I do a lot of things right that I never saw before because our Core Wound/Negative Ego was dominating our thought process with nothing but lies before we even knew better! I get it right all the time by being loyal, honest, dedicated, intelligent, intuitive, saying yes to going on a retreat where I found our Core Wound," etc…. Imagine how your Inner Child would feel then, knowing this happens in her future! She might not know the concept of money, but she would know that she could dream endless dreams of all the possibilities that her life could be and that her Future Self is her reliable and true superhero that stopped the lies and the feelings associated with them, and that most of her dreams would actually come true! Your Core Wound would become an obsolete and absolute lie! This example is an actual true story of a client that was a multimillionaire at twenty-nine who couldn't think of anything to put down on her preliminary list of what's right with her – and she had good looks, good health, great brain, great everything!

It's amazing how we can become steeped in our Negative Ego/Core Wound so much that we can't even see the obvious truth *at all.* It's like our Negative Ego creates a force field around us that won't let the truth in, bouncing off any compliments or self-esteem, because it doesn't fit our self-image, template, ICOS. If you've ever watched the movie, *It's a Wonderful Life,* you've seen the character played by Jimmy Stewart be saturated throughout the film by his Negative Ego. It isn't until the last scene in the movie that he finally gets shown and realizes the truth, his Negative Ego finally gets busted, and his life changes forever, free from the agony of his own worst enemy, which almost caused him to jump off a bridge!

***

That was a taste in preparation for the next step.

Again, now that you realize how much pain you're causing your own Inner Child (and you), it's time to take your Negative Ego to court. You are now going to be the Prosecuting Attorney, and you have to convince the Judge that your Negative Ego has to be put away for life never to have any influence over you ever again. This means you have to use **FACTS – specific ones -** for real proof because *general affirmations do not work.*

General affirmations do not work!

You have already started to get the hang of it by writing down positive general statements about yourself. Now it's time to take it all the way.

In a different colored ink, write down the facts in between the lies you've already written down in black on the worksheet. Be specific; use names, real accomplishments, and/or real-life experiences, etc.

General affirmations won't even come close to proving your case, and your Negative Ego will make a mockery of you if you use them. As an example, if you have written a lie down such as, "No one will ever understand you" and you refute it with, "I am now understood by everyone I want," your Negative Ego will say (subconsciously), "Yeah, right, how you gonna do that, and who is it? You can't even connect with anyone! Your own husband and mother don't even understand you. Your kids don't understand you, and the people at work don't even care! You feel alone all the time you dumbass." You need proof; you need names, even if it's that friend from fourth grade (that at least gets rid of the word "ever" in the lie), and then move on from there, even if it's only your own Inner Child, Soul, God, Higher Self, or Future Self that understands you. Surely you have at least one best friend, too?

A lot of people have Negative Egos that say "You're stupid." To refute with facts write something like, "I won the spelling bee in third grade" (just write: spelling bee), "I won a scholarship for college," (write: college scholarship), "Raised two great kids," "Got a B.A./3.8 GPA," "Been promoted at work four times."

The Negative Ego can't argue with any of that; it was there and witnessed it all and knows it's all true. Now that it knows you know the truth and won't accept its lies anymore, your Negative Ego will just slink away; it will slink back to its room way back in the back of your mind, knowing that it can't get away with lying to you anymore, knowing that you're conscious of the factual truth and will no longer listen to its habitual, stupid, harmful and hurtful lies. You'll set you and your Inner Child free from all your mental/emotional pain and start growing new neuropathways that will rewire your brain and create an entirely new life inwardly and outwardly, also all supported with new and greatly improved emotional peptides. The cell receptors for the old emotional peptides of your ICOS/Template, Core Wound neuropathway superhighways will eventually completely atrophy – and sooner than you imagine, according to your willpower.

Worksheet, Example 2

Core Wound: "_____I am not wanted._____."

Since your Core Wound is the Lie, your Negative Ego is the Liar. Your Negative Ego (negative self-image) is the subconscious voice of your Core Wound. _Every time_ you are feeling the primary emotions of your Core Wound, your Negative Ego is subconsciously telling you the lies of your Core Wound.

List the primary emotions of your core wound:

_____Sad_____   _____Anxious_____   _____Insecure_____

This is what determines your inner and outer reactive thoughts, feelings, behavior, beliefs and much more (the "Twelve") until you consciously choose otherwise. You must know what your Negative Ego says to you in order to become conscious enough of it to choose otherwise and deactivate your Negative Ego's influence. IN BETWEEN THE LINES OF LIES, WRITE THE FACTUAL TRUTH IN RED INK (italicized here). TELL THE TRUTH WITH CONSCIOUS, SPECIFIC *FACTS*; OTHERWISE, THE NEGATIVE EGO WILL MAKE A MOCKERY OF GENERAL AFFIRMATIONS AND WIN ITS "CASE" EVERY TIME.

1. **You're stupid.** *Got BA/3.8 GPA, married love of my life, got promoted four times, won essay contest. Intuitive and can read ppl instantly (Joe, Burt, Carrie...). They call me MacGyver!*

2. **You'll never have any friends.** *Greg, Lance, Judith, Renee, Art, Maya, Ralph. Great connections in other countries (Franc, Huber, Katzman, Foster). Neighborhood loves me.*
3. **You'll never be successful.** *Promoted 4x, pd off house, married 25 yrs, great kids/father, soccer champs, host annual July 4th celebrations at lake. Can retire easy! Healed addiction.*
4. *You'll never fit in. Am an AA sponsor, assistant soccer coach, have great in-laws, men's group, July 4 party. Nat. Guard. Captain of football team. Referee chess tournaments.*
5. **People only take advantage of you.** *In-laws co-signed our 1st house, boss got me my 1st promotion, ppl take care of me at home/work (Carla, MJ) and 7/4.* (Note: Heal codep!)
6. **You're better off alone.** *Family/in-laws really help out! Gave us firewood & food. Rushed me to hospital.* (Note: Need to heal CODA, have healthy boundaries.) **My wife is a total gift!**
7. **You're such a phony.** *Saved wife's life from drowning, protected daughters, fired ppl at work. Those were real. Have cried in public, spoke at funeral.* (Note: Heal CODA.) *I'm an HSP!*

You can probably now easily do twenty more lies; the more the better in order to become conscious of all of your Negative Ego's lies. It is a life-long bad habit, an emotional addiction, and your "comfort zone." Always refute the lies with truth based on specific FACTS, so your Negative Ego can't argue; if you give your Negative Ego any room to argue, it will win.

The better you are with facts, and an abundance of them, the easier it will be to neutralize your Negative Ego. Don't let your Negative Ego take any cookies out of the cookie jar! The cookies are the Lies the Negative Ego feasts upon; it has been feasting upon them nearly all your life, and it's addicted to them (the emotional peptides). Every time your Negative Ego reaches into the cookie jar to eat and spew out another lie, tell it to put that damn cookie back! Quit eating the lies! Another way to put it is quit watering the weeds! That's why we have to identify the cookies or weeds first, so we can consciously catch ourselves telling those lies to ourselves and stop doing it.

Though it's with us for life, we can consciously correct our Core Wound/Lie by means of busting our Negative Ego/Liar, thereby putting it into permanent retirement or "inactive duty." Mine's on permanent mental disability. If it ever tries to come up and test me, first I tell it, "Do you want me to tell you what I already know you're going to say?" It knows I know it so well that I won't let it get away with convincing me of its lies, so it just slinks away, as I tell it to go enjoy its disability benefits and go watch its favorite cartoons. I tell it it doesn't have to work anymore. At all. I've disabled it. I'm onto it, and it knows I know it is a 100 percent liar at all times and has zero words of self-love to offer. There is never a good reason to *ever* listen to our Negative Ego.

There is never a good reason to *ever* listen to your Negative Ego.

This has cured me forever of depression and rage, which I have proven for over two decades now. The void caused by losing those two reactive, habitual emotions has simultaneously allowed me to consciously place myself within the spectrum of habitual joy, and, when I was finally ready, it was a genuine commitment ceremony (to joy) that instantly transformed me. To have permanently and consciously changed my "Twelve" from the spectrum of chronic depression to the spectrum of chronic joy is one of my biggest personal miracles. If I can do it, you can do it.

I changed "the backdrop of my stage" by knowing my Core Wound is a Lie, and I re-trained myself out of my Negative Ego's influence with consciousness and willpower. Doing so is now called neuroplasticity: consciously creating new neuropathways in our brain and letting the old neuropathways atrophy along with the starving cell receptors associated with those previous peptides that were connected to the Lie. It's easier than you think; it only takes consciousness and the persistence of willpower and the map I've created here to show you how, so it won't have to take you nearly as long as it did me.

Getting back to the concept of "the backdrop of my stage...." Imagine you're in a theater watching a play; there's always a backdrop for the entire stage for each act or scene the actors play in. The backdrop is to set a theme or a mood for whatever's being played out on stage. It's the same in real life: until healed, our personal backdrop - our outlook on life - is determined by our Core Wound and its theme or mood, the resonance of our "Twelve." The thing is, the very same things are happening on the real-world stage at all times, both good and bad such as falling in love, that nasty divorce, that unfair business failure, that loved one who died, our job... but our own personal backdrop determines how we feel about it and react to it. We, with our Core Wound backdrop, are affected by its "Twelve." Some will be pissed off about what's going on "onstage" while others will love what's going on, or be sad, scared, humored, or anxious, etc. All I'm saying is that if I can change my backdrop from gloomy, heavy depression to laughter, fun, and joy, so can you.

By healing our Core Wound, changing our backdrop is a fundamental, profound shift to make. And no one else can do it for us. That's the good news, because it means we don't have to rely on anyone else to make it happen*!* That means the person that sexually abused us, for instance, can't do it for us - if they're even still alive. Mom, dad, guru, or whoever – even lover - can't do it for us. The power to change is solely in our own hands. It's the wanting for others to do it that's the problem, as if childishly expecting, even demanding, that others have to right the wrong they did to us. Good luck with that strategy, I think we've already been waiting for "lifetimes" for that to happen. Even ones that love us can only support us to heal our own Core Wound/Lie and Negative Ego/Liar, but they will never be able to do it for us.

The power to change is solely up to you.

We mustn't let our Negative Ego trick us into believing we've got it all done and never have to worry about it again, either. It's like the Terminator (from the movie starring Arnold Schwarzenegger): our Negative Ego will keep coming back if we let it, so we can't neglect being ever-vigilant of it, at least until we have a very good personal understanding of it, enough to put it into permanent retirement. Even then, we must stay functionally conscious of it and maintain the new programming we've done to ourselves. We can't fake or falsely believe that we've healed our Core Wound or Negative Ego until it's actually true because that doesn't work. Our Negative Ego would love for us to fake it because then it could still effortlessly run the show.

The Negative Ego is also our worst self-saboteur: "You don't need to heal anything. Your life's fine. You're better off than most. The Core Wound's not real. It can't be that easy to heal. Nothing's wrong with you, you don't even need to look into it. Focusing on what's wrong is for losers. Forget the past, just focus on the future. Your childhood wasn't that bad; even if it was, it's all over, forget about it. Why go back into some kind of wound or whatever? In fact, if you focus on your wound, it's just going to increase it, you know, that law of attraction thing." Our Negative Ego can go on all day and night like that mostly at a subconscious level.

In addition, many people misunderstand "that law of attraction thing." One way to define denial is lack of attention, but lack of attention doesn't work in healing your Core Wound. Many think that if they give certain bad things (such as the Core Wound) too much attention they will manifest more of it into their lives, but your Core Wound exists whether you give it attention or not. It takes focus, intention, commitment, attention – i.e. willpower – to heal the ICOS with consciousness. You have a Core Wound that operates in the shadows, and it is your job to shed light (consciousness) upon it. You can't just leave it unattended and expect your life to change the way you want it to. It's not enough just to know what your Core Wound is. The whole point of knowing it is to be able to do something about it. It is your Negative Ego that does not understand this and doesn't want to do anything about it. The last thing your Negative Ego wants is to have its work change, as it's very easy for it to run the show on automatic, the subconscious. Since you have to become conscious of your Core Wound and Negative Ego in order to overrun the subconscious, you must give your Negative Ego a lot of attention. Remember, your "Twelve" is the overall resonance of your being, and that resonance *is* your main attractor. You don't want denial to be part of it.

The resonance of your "Twelve" *is* your main law of attraction.

Our Core Wound is part of what's called our shadow self, the part of our psyche that resides in the darkness of our subconscious and unconscious. The Core Wound is the underworld of our own personal psyche; it is the Kore Wall on the dark side of Mt. Everest that's in permanent shadow, our own personal underworld, and our Negative

Ego runs the place. It runs the place until we are able and willing enough to shine the light of consciousness on it.

For those that believe they already "have it all," they can be fooled into thinking that they don't need to heal their Core Wound. There's nothing wrong with "having it all," but our Negative Ego will never take us where it's letting us think we're going with all that success because our Negative Ego is always part of our Lower Self. Once we've healed enough of our Negative Ego and Lower Self by addressing our Core Wound, we can have all the same success with authenticity and real spirituality. Rather than allowing our success to feed our ego, why not let our success come from our Higher Self? Our Higher Self is most connected with spirituality, that personal relationship with "God/Goddess/All That Is," G/G/A. Our Lower Self is most connected to our Negative Ego, which is about as far away from G/G/A as we can get. Our physical riches can be the same either way, but the tragic way is to allow our Negative Ego to trick us into ultimate spiritual failure.

Our Negative Ego is always part of our Lower Self, our weak shadow self.

Along the way, sometimes a one-liner comes along that can change our life; one of them for me was, "If you don't know what to do to heal, at *least* stop doing what doesn't work." What a no-brainer, right? But I had to hear it from someone. Just stop doing what you already know doesn't work! The void that's created by doing so will be filled by something better every time, and you don't need to know beforehand what the replacement will be.

If you don't know what to do to heal, at *least* stop doing what doesn't work*!*

Learn to identify your Negative Ego so you can stop listening to it, and counter it with factual truth!

Another great input a client gave to this work was the realization that, if you read the Negative Ego's lies back to your Negative Ego (rather doing it to your Inner Child and yourself), then all of the statements become true! For instance, the seven lies used in the previous worksheet example are true for the Negative Ego: "*You* are stupid! *You'll* never have any friends. *You'll* never be successful. *You'll* never fit in. *You* only take advantage of *me* (variation). *You're* better off alone." That *is* true for your Negative Ego but not for any other part of yourself.

***

Here's a final thought for this chapter and an important reiteration. The most crucial part of healing your Core Wound is creating a new habit of telling yourself the truth about yourself rather than continuing to listen to your Negative Ego's subconscious lies. Become conscious of your Negative Ego's lies, and then you can refute that voice with conscious truth. The crucial part is you must become very good at telling yourself the truth, *especially in the moment* when your Negative

Ego is lying. What I gave you in the above exercise where you wrote the factual truth between the lines of the lies you read to your Inner Child was just a short example. You want to expand upon the truths as much as you can. This literally begins to reprogram your brain with new neuropathways. Get used to countering the lies until you don't even have to, when the neuropathways of the Negative Ego/Liar start to atrophy, as the new neuropathways based on truth are growing. You're in for a great surprise - just wait till those new neuropathways begin to grow into your limbic brain (our emotional brain), which literally change your emotions and memories, your story, all which spring from your conscious truth. Those old, lie-supporting pathways can be reconstituted like fat cells getting plump again, so you must remain vigilant, but by telling yourself the ever-improving truth, your consciously altered subconscious power becomes ever more automatic.

People often ask me how long it will take to heal their Core Wound. The answer is: how strong is your will power (commitment and persistence) to do this book's process and how well can you specifically tell your Negative Ego the truth so that all it can say is, "Oh yeah, you're right," and just slink away? What if you got beyond the important details of the truth to be able to always have your subconscious truth be, "I am a miracle of life!" (One doesn't even have to believe in God for that one, so everyone could say that one). "Simply because I'm alive I have a purpose, and a primary purpose is to heal my Core Wound because it's the biggest blockage in my life from creating my dreams (or even being able to have any). Lined up end-to-end, my body has at least 600 miles of nerve cells, 100 billion of which are in my brain," etc. (The more you learn about your body, the more miraculous you become, such as a full DNA molecule exists within every cell of your body and unwinds to be three feet long, and that there are 500 to 2,000 individual mitochondria within each cell, all with their own DNA separate from your human cell). Yet the pain and symptoms of one's Core Wound causes some to take ultimately lethal drugs? Or become an alcoholic? Or have a toxic attitude enough to cause physical ailments and lousy situations? And your Negative Ego's the cause! It's so tragic it's laughable!

How about becoming a healthy cell in the body of humanity by healing yourself instead of one of the ever-increasing cancer cells (Negative Ego world) in that body? You already have the traits of being a good person just by reading this far; would a bad person (someone with a lot of unhealed pain and unwilling to heal) have even bothered to buy the book or get through the introduction, or care about being a positive influence? Give yourself a break and tell that Negative Ego to shut the eff up and why what it has been saying isn't even true!

Anyway, get really good at your inner truth telling! At first it might feel uncomfortable because you're also going to start having a new self-image, a new Identity, and an all-new resonance from your "Twelve," with new neuropathways and new peptides supporting them, so just remember that:

All healing is outside your comfort zone until you "rewire" yourself.

That new you is based upon the truth of who you really are.

CHAPTER 4
SUPPORT

I mentioned in the introduction that mutually knowing our Core Wound with someone we're in a primary relationship with will greatly increase our ability to help each other heal and create more love, fun, and consciousness together. Knowing each other's Core Wound allows us the opportunity to address each other in language and behavior tailored to help heal each other's Wound rather than to unintentionally and reactively "throw salt" in it and then further react in pain towards each other. Rather than bug one another, we can learn to support our partner to "de-bug" themselves (you can't heal someone else's Core Wound; you can only support them by helping them stay conscious of doing so) by learning the love language of the Core Wound.

Let's start off with what I call a Communication Ceremony. This of course is for your primary relationship, such as your spouse or "life-partner," but also can be done with other family members or deepest friendships, etc.

Imagine how wedding vows are done: stand face-to-face, look at one another in the eyes (without glasses) and be present with each other. Focus on your breath and your partner's eyes. You can hold hands if you want, but it's usually better if you don't because it might be too distracting for one of you.

One of you is going to start by asking the other a certain question, and the other answers the question in one or two words. The first person then asks the same question, and the other answers with a different answer. You repeat this about ten times, and the answers are meant to come out quick without too much thought, since they are meant to come from your heart as best you can.

The first question is, "What do you love about me?" It's important to ask the question each time, too, because it is actually hard for some to even ask that particular question. Some even diminish the word love to, "What do you like about me?" since the thought of being loveable is too outside their comfort zone or self-esteem. Don't do that. When you've asked and answered several times, it's time for the questioner to repeat as many of the answers as they can remember (hopefully all of them because they were fully present... but you don't have to be perfect). Then you trade roles and repeat the process with the other person questioning with the same question and the former questioner now being the one who answers.

Do the same process with different questions, such as, "What do you fear?" That's a good one; you might be very surprised with what you hear. Another is, "What are you sad about?" And, "What's one thing you want me to know about you that I don't know?" You can come up with your own questions, but they must not be manipulative; this is supposed to be a ceremony of safety, vulnerability, and heart-opening.

I remember the first time I had a couple ask each other, "What do you fear?" They had been married for thirty years, and many of the answers were new to each other; they had no idea what their partner feared and had never thought of even asking nor saying. They got to know one another like they never had in all that time and both cried their eyes out and bonded together in a deeper way than ever.

"What's one thing you want me to know about you that I don't know?" is a question I've seen save marriages. For instance, the answer for one wife was, "You have no idea how much I always just want to feel safe." She had always been too afraid to even say that before, and her husband really didn't know. She also had just discovered her Core Wound was "I'm not safe." Now that it was out, and with a lot more tears for both of them, it profoundly changed everything. His Core Wound was, "I'm on my own," and his answer to the question was, "I just want you to know how lonely I am *all the time*." Now he realized all he had to do was make her feel safe, which he genuinely wanted to do out of love for her. Feeling safe about him would cause her to want to bond with him, and the more she bonded with him the more it would heal the loneliness that came with his own Wound. Until you heal your Core Wound, the dynamic tends to work backwards, and that's why people have problems: the adult-adapted ICOS.

The lack of communication can cause such loneliness in people, followed with the behavioral acting out that comes as a result, which is the cause of so much pain. For example, lack of communication or of good communication is by far the number one cause of infidelity. Before this couple had come to find out their Core Wound, he had acted out this way because of feeling disconnected and lonely, which made her feel unsafe and withdraw, which made him feel even lonelier, etc. Before the affair, he had always felt lonely and she had always felt unsafe, but because they didn't communicate well, they didn't even know that about one another, yet it was directly from each of their Core Wounds, which was their subconscious normal and familiar comfort zone but also their longest-standing, deepest pain since childhood. It seems most people want to hide their deepest pain from their partner, and though it doesn't make sense (…well, it's shame…), the fear, vulnerability and shame of opening up is understandable. It's just too bad hiding your deepest pain doesn't work.

Most people never even think to realize that people primarily get married to heal together. Especially as the pyramid of needs (Maslow's hierarchy of needs) are met.

Unlike the other questions, this question - "What's one thing you want me to know about you that I don't know?" - only needs to be asked once when that rare time might come up to ask it. In the case above, it was a very tender moment with such realization about one another that the understanding it provided opened their minds, their hearts, and their commitment to love one another again like new – and deeper. Forgiveness comes more when the "why" is understood about what someone did more than the "what."

It's hard to imagine anyone wanting to split up with their partner if they have mutually healed their Core Wounds together.

***

Now you are ready for the Communication Ceremony for the love language of the Core Wound. Rather than asking, "What do you love about me?", you can ask them according to their Core Wound such as, "How are you important?" or, "How are you wanted?" or "How are you worthy?" and so on. Your loved one is the one that needs to get good at answering this. Some really struggle at first. But remember, each neuron in our brain is connected to 10,000 other neurons, so it doesn't take too long to get comfortable with new neuropathways. And it helps tremendously to have some support along the way! Make it fun and rewarding!

This is to be specifically about your loved one's Core Wound. They would ask, for example, "How am I loveable?" (if "I am unloveable" is their Core Wound). Then you would answer in a short phrase or less. The first would then ask again, "How am I loveable?" You would give another, different short answer. You could do this about ten times. Then you trade and repeat the process: you would ask your partner, "How am I wanted?" (if "I am not wanted" is your Core Wound), and they would answer in a short phrase or less, repeating the process about ten times. You can do this process once a day, once week or whenever you want.

You want to make it a new habit to use this new language. If you know what your partner's Core Wound is - "I don't matter," for example - you want to tell them how they matter often and on a random but regular basis, *and be specific*. Tell them daily throughout each day. You can also *ask them* how they matter. Reminding one another with such support goes a long way. There's nothing wrong with reminding one another to keep telling your Negative Ego/Liar the truth until the new habit takes over with those new neuropathways you're each developing. It doesn't take long. Pretty soon you'll be laughing about it instead of subconsciously triggering each other and bickering over every little thing.

About that bickering. We probably all know what it's like when two Negative Egos are in battle with each other, triggering and reacting back and forth into that very quick downward spiral that occurs. Times like that are what I call a Negative Ego Brain Storm, a NEBS, because negative thoughts and feelings about your partner completely take over your brain even more than what you negatively think and feel about yourself (until you've healed your Core Wound). Unless consciously intercepted, a NEBS can go on up to every waking moment of the day until a relationship ends – and then some.

You have already discovered how painful it is to your Inner Child to hear the Negative Ego's lies from their Future Self when you read those lies to them to get the impact of what you were and are doing to yourself. But the statements that come out of the NEBS you have toward your spouse/partner are even worse! And it becomes an obsession. I know because sometimes I have couples write them out; instead of the Negative Ego lies you wrote about yourself these are about your partner. They're so bad that I never let partners see what each one's Negative Ego is saying about their partner. That would ruin everything! People would go to prison if they acted out on some of the things they let their NEBS say internally. I only have people do this so they can see in their own writing how toxic their Negative Ego is towards their partner and how absurdly obvious it is that it will never make a relationship work – quite the opposite! I'm not even going to print some of the NEBS statements in this book! (And some clients wonder why I laugh…. I definitely make sure those statements are ripped up, buried, burned, and/or smashed to bits with big rocks. If we're in a room for some rare reason, I have them rip them up and one at a time go into the bathroom to flush them down the loo.)

You must also realize by now, obviously, that what you say to your partner is also what you're saying to their Inner Child. It's similar to you allowing your Negative Ego to say bad things to your own Inner Child. You have experienced what that does to you, so it should be no surprise as to what it does to your partner. It is so much better to be conscious enough to address their Inner Child (Higher Self and Future Self would nice, too) than to bash them with your own Negative Ego. Again, don't become their personified Negative Ego to them nor vise-versa.

What you say to your partner goes directly into their Inner Child, too.

That said, imagine the difference when you consciously stop the NEBS towards your partner by incorporating the love language of the Core Wound with each other. Imagine you both get triggered, and you're starting to go down that familiar path. It only takes one of you to snap out of it and say, "You know what I love about you?" Or, "You matter too much to me to let us do this (NEBS) to each other." "You matter to me because you're the most intelligent woman I've ever known, and you're truly the best mother our kids could ever have." "You matter so much to me that for love's sake I'm going to change (fill in the blank: whatever words or behavior of mine that I know doesn't work)." That can stop an argument in its tracks and start bringing some consciousness and heart-opening into the fray.

You want to keep yourself on the path of healing your Core Wound and support your partner with the opportunity to do the same. You're already probably an expert in doing the opposite, so you don't need to do that anymore.

Of course, the love language of the Core Wound applies to all the Core Wounds. If the other person's Core Wound is, "I'm not important," get used to telling them all the time how they are important, and also ask them how they are important from time to time. If it's, "I'm not valued," get used to telling them how you value them, etc. Or why she is more important than anyone else, or why he deserves love, or how she gets things right, or how he's acceptable the way he is, etc. It will change both your worlds. You will help change your loved one's neuropathways and help them do so for themselves as well. Plus it's just a great habit to have if you want to have a more loving, more conscious relationship that's also going to be a *lot* more fun.

The point is, be specific in addressing their own personal Core Wound. If their Core Wound is, "I'm not enough," it won't even come close to helping them to say, "You're perfect for me because I love that you have slightly crooked teeth like me (perhaps for the Core Wound "I am flawed"), and how cute your forgetfulness is, and that you don't care if your clothes don't fit right and how slightly disheveled your hair always is. I love all that, and it's a huge turn-on for me because who you are makes me so comfortable and grateful to be with you...." All that might not help at all to the "I'm not enough" person as much as saying, "I can't believe how much you gave of yourself today; I mean first you give me a surprise invite and treat in the shower together, then you took care of the kids when it was my turn to do it, you go to work and make record sales for the company, get back in time to take your mother to her doctor appointment, plan a nice little trip out of town just for us together, cook dinner, and partially rearrange your home office. Who else can do stuff like that all day every day? I love you like crazy, you're amazing. It would take at least two people to keep up with you."

A NEBS, on the other hand, will keep any and all of that away from one another, vanished.

There are a few Core Wounds in which words don't mean much at all. "No one cares, I'm on my own, I'm not safe, I'm not safe enough, I'm not wanted, and I don't belong" all need physical actions or demonstrations to take place much more than words. It's not that the other Wounds don't need action, it's that these Wounds listed definitely do. Only actions mean anything to these particular Wounds because words might sound nice – it's better than nothing and a good start – but only actions will make a difference.

As an example, for me, one time my partner made muffins for me and put walnuts in them (so simple, I know…), but the thing is, she didn't like muffins and didn't like walnuts at all, but she knew I loved both, so the fact that she even made muffins and then even remembered to put walnuts in them made a huge difference, memorable to this day. Why? Because she was proving she cared! That's why I felt so loved just by her randomly making muffins with walnuts. I know it seems ridiculous, but often the littlest things make the biggest difference (remember? - **Love pays attention to detail**) especially for Wounds that need action more than words. If such little things can be so big for some of the Wounds, imagine how big of a difference the big things make! Like supportive, more meaningful communication – ideally on all echelons: mental, emotional, physical, spiritual.

***

There are some other systems that fit very well with healing one's Core Wound. The following are some of the more substantial ones I've delved into in order to heal myself. Like I said in the introduction, I discovered my Core Wound by doing the "long division." This was after I healed Codependence, Martyrdom, Shame, Reactive Attachment Disorder and many other things. I was never a Narcissist, but it was something I had to deal with until I understood why narcissists came into my life; then I could heal the underlying issue. After I discovered my Core Wound, it made sense of all the other issues I'd had to heal; my Core Wound was the underlying cause of them all. Had I known my Core Wound first, though I have no regrets (it was part of and led to my destiny, after all) it may have sped up my process by several years.

CODEPENDENCE

Codependence basically means that you don't have a life of your own, so what you do with your life is ultimately based upon what other people want and even come to expect or demand of you from your consistent enabling of them. As a default, you end up living your life in support of others because you don't know what you want for yourself. Your life becomes one of weakness and cowardice (ouch) because you can't say no to people, or if you do you feel guilt. You avoid upsetting or disappointing people because you're afraid of having to stand up for yourself, but you have nothing to stand up for because you don't have a life. You have no hobbies, and you don't have fun of your own. You are codependent because you want people to like you, so as an overcompensation of your Core Wound you have become a people pleaser as a habit and always put yourself second at best or last at worst.

Codependency fits a lot of Core Wounds. For example, "I am not important, I'm not good enough, I don't matter, no one cares," are only four out of the list. You want people to care about you or to feel that you matter or that you're good enough or are important, so you go out of your way to care for others more than yourself, make sure they feel good enough, that they matter, and that *they're* more important even than yourself. In other words, you give them what you want for yourself, but it doesn't work that way. You get taken advantage of all the time and feel resentful, yet it's your own fault! And deep down you know it.

It is significant to know that being codependent has a commonality with alcoholism, as CODA meetings (Codependence Anonymous) originated as an offshoot of AA meetings (Alcoholics Anonymous), based on the Twelve Steps. This is indicative of how much being codependent can ruin your life.

It was revealed that a lot of people are codependent who live with alcoholics because their life revolves around the alcoholic's mood swings and abusive behavior. A codependent does not want to trigger or be a victim of that, so "turns themself into a pretzel" to avoid that, and then is always "walking on eggshells" as a result. In other words, their life revolves around the alcoholic. However, one does not have to be in a relationship with an addict to become codependent; it's more about your Core Wound that's subconsciously causing you to be codependent whether it's with an addict or not.

The following list is a partial list of the traits of a codependent person. The first trait fits the layman's definition of codependency perfectly:

- We tend to put other peoples' wants and needs before our own.
- We tend to fear and/or worry how other may respond to our feelings.
- We are afraid of being hurt and/or rejected by others.
- We have difficulty making decisions.
- We tend to minimize, alter or even deny the truth about how we feel.
- Other peoples' actions and attitudes tend to determine how we react.
- Our fear of others' feelings (anger, hurt...) determines what we say or do.
- We value others' opinions more than our own.
- Their struggle affects our serenity.

- Our mental attention is focused on pleasing others.
- We have no hobbies or interests of our own; we go along with theirs.
- I'm not aware of what I want; I ask what you want.
- My social circle diminishes as I involve myself with you.
- I put my values aside in order to connect with you.
- I am unable to say no and do not have healthy boundaries.

If you have even half of these traits, you are codependent. If you are, healing codependency is *__MANDATORY HEALING__* because not enough is going to change in your life until you heal this pattern. Healing codependency will also greatly accelerate the healing of your Core Wound, but if you don't do it, it won't.

You also have some fundamental human rights that are good to know:

- You have a right to have personal boundaries
- You have a right to say no without feeling guilty
- You have a right to take care of yourself
- You have a right to protect yourself
- You have a right to have healthy relationships
- You have a right to be your true self
- You have a right to heal yourself

If you're codependent you need to come up with at least one or two hobbies and interests because you don't have any, which gives you no reason to say no to people who want something of you. With no hobbies nor your own interests, you are indicating to people that your life and your time is not as important as theirs.

Your hobbies and your interests go hand-in-hand with fun, so it would also empower you to make a Fun List, a list of ten things that are fun to do that don't necessarily require anyone else's participation. A list of ten things that would be fun to do that would make you happy, period. Happiness is a personal responsibility. If your happiness depends on what another person does or doesn't do (fun or not), you are codependent.

Happiness is a personal responsibility!

A very powerful statement for a codependent person to learn to say when someone is asking of them something they don't want to do is simply to say, "That doesn't work for me." If you have to make it easier for yourself you can say, "That doesn't work for me right now."

"That doesn't work for me right now."

Remember, "we teach people how to treat us!" Remember, your resonance has your Core Wound metaphorically stamped on your forehead for everyone to see. And realize that no one else has a problem saying no except a codependent.

As for the Fun List, how difficult was it for you to even come up with ten things? But now, go through your list and checkmark all the things you've done in the past two weeks. Amazingly, most people check half or less. If you could only check five, write "50%" off to the side of your list. If you were in school that would equal an "E"; you are failing at having fun – because you're codependent. Even "60%" is a "D," and "70%" is only a "C." How hard is it, really, to do all ten things on that list in fourteen days? How hard is it to get an "A"? Plenty of people do, and it's very doubtful they're codependent. What you want to do is update your Fun List at least every two weeks until you have 8, 9, or 10 things on there that you actually do at least once every fourteen days, and be honest with yourself. For instance, is "going to the gym" *actually* fun? Maybe it is, maybe it's not; the question is, does it honestly belong on that list? The point of this is that codependent people are not happy people. They probably put on a good face and pretend they are, but they actually carry a lot of resentment or depression and maybe even jealousy or envy. A codependent person needs to make themselves happy.

Again, like anything else, it only takes consciousness and willpower to heal anything. Become conscious of what codependence is by reading books, researching on the Internet, and going to CODA meetings. Do not think you can avoid going to CODA meetings; they are way more impactful than reading books or the Internet. It is your Negative Ego that thinks you don't need to go and does not want to go and probably tells you that it is beneath you to attend. How honestly do you truly want to heal? Remember, your Negative Ego is your worst enemy*!* You might even find out, at least for a while, that going to CODA meetings goes on your Fun List!

***

MARTYR

Being codependent can easily lead to becoming a martyr, which might be a magnitude worse. And yes, this is another big thing I had to heal.

The traits of a martyr:

- Feel unappreciated
- Misunderstood
- Hopeless
- Helpless
- Burdened with too much responsibility (& chronic resentment)
- Saddled with too many problems unable to solve
- Blamed for things you didn't do

A martyr is in a constant state of a Negative Ego Brain Storm (NEBS) toward life with a full-on addiction to the peptides of their Core Wound. This makes one a chronic complainer, expectant of nothing ever working, resentful, tired, etc. There is plenty of information out there on how to heal this, just search "how to heal being a martyr" on the Internet to start.

If it comes up in my sessions with clients, I give them a good dose of the first awareness of what it is. One is, the only other people that hang around a martyr for long is another martyr. It must be where that old saying comes from of "Misery loves company," but it's definitely not a fun life. If you are a martyr, you deserve better, and it's a must to heal if you're ever going to be happy. Martyrs have a victim mentality, and healthy relationships are not built upon someone having an investment in being a victim. Healing martyrdom is also a big step in healing many of the Core Wounds martyrdom can be part of.

***

ATTACHMENT DISORDER
(NOT Attachment Style!)

How to heal attachment disorder is the subject of my next book. But just to touch upon it here, attachment disorder is a silent, largely unaddressed societal epidemic that even many counselors and therapists still don't know about, let alone how to heal it if they do.

When I get clients, both men and women, who have cheated on their partner, it's likely (but not a given) they are somewhere on the spectrum of attachment disorder, or they probably wouldn't have cheated in the first place. This disorder comes from our childhood programming, set in our subconscious or even deeper, as our nervous system never got accustomed to what it's like to be healthily bonded to someone. This means we didn't grow up with some combination of affection, nurturing, or protection, for instance, but did grow up with physical abuse, neglect, abandonment, and/or major illness, and so on. As a result, certain neuropathways throughout our body and brain never got connected at a physical, emotional or psychological level. Attachment Disorder makes people deeply feel that they're on their own, so it also fits a lot of the Core Wounds.

Attachment Disorder, until only ten to twenty years ago, was mostly only diagnosed for children. The fact that unhealed kids grow up to be unhealed adults with attachment disorder (adult-adapted attachment disorder) seems to have never even been considered until then. Even now there are very few books written about it, and only one book has been written by someone who has actually had Reactive Attachment Disorder that I'm aware of.[7]

At age forty-two, I realized I had Reactive Attachment Disorder (what used to be called RAD Syndrome, which is way up there on the spectrum, beyond "normal" attachment disorder). As I had already experienced twelve years of deep and successful healing, I immediately set to healing it. I didn't heal RAD by reading books about it nor having some college degree nor special training in it nor even having a therapist of any sort. I did it with plenty of spiritual help (a personal relationship with a Higher Power – a generic way of putting it….), big and genuine commitments to self to heal, and more willpower than I ever realized I had, and a lot of consciousness, introspection, and observation of my behavior. (Remember? If you don't know what to do to heal, at least stop doing what doesn't work!)

Since then, from what I have investigated about it on the Internet, though there is worthwhile information on it now, attachment disorder also seems to have been reduced to an overly complicated fractionalization that's not helpful and even confuses the issue (such as "disinhibited, oppositional-defiant, anxious-ambivalent, anxious-avoidant, and more" attachment STYLES, not disorders). It seems that people have over-analyzed it because the ones studying it don't understand it because they never had it. As far as I know, experts still say that RAD cannot be healed. I can tell you from having had it that it can be healed. Like anything else, it takes consciousness and willpower. And I am constantly improving my healing of it. Remember? **Vulneratus non Victus!**

There are a lot of symptoms to attachment disorder besides the ones mentioned here, so stay tuned. I hope to have it out within a year from when this book you're reading is published.

Here are the sheets I use "in the field" for a taste:

ATTACHMENT DISORDER is caused when one's nervous system was not programmed to have the innate ability to bond with others, where affection is foreign, and one feels they're on their own (including subconsciously and unconsciously). Attachment disorder is on a continuum that ranges from less severe attachment issues - such as loneliness, anger, depression, and distrust - all the way to Reactive Attachment Disorder, in which all that and more is amplified.

HERE'S A LIST OF SYMPTOMS TO TEST YOURSELF WITH:

- Difficulty handling conflict with others, argumentative
- Denial of or no responsibility for wrong-doing
- Control others by overtly hostile or manipulative ways
- Trouble showing empathy, remorse, trust, or compassion
- Lack of the ability to give or receive genuine affection or love

- Sex with another is still just self-gratification compared to what's possible (which is unknown)
- True intimacy is unknown, uncomfortable, foreign, and/or causes anxiety
- Resistance to efforts by others to nurture or guide you
- Emotionally self-absorbed
- Lacks cause and effect thinking, impulsive, lacks self-control
- Provokes anger in others and acts out negatively
- Lies, cheats, manipulates, or steals
- Can be destructive and cruel
- Tend to "ghost" friends and lovers
- Superficially engaging or charming
- Behaves in anger to protect feelings of sadness or fear
- Feels isolated and depressed
- Feels frustrated and stressed
- Addictive behavior such as substance abuse, and/or work, gambling, or sex addiction, etc.
- Behaves hyper-vigilantly, agitated, and/or has trouble concentrating
- Confused, puzzled, and obsessed with finding answers
- Feels blamed by family and friends or even therapists
- Feels hopeless, helpless, and angry
- Feels misunderstood, even by self

You would be shocked by how many checkmarks people make. It's kind of like being pregnant: you either are or you aren't. AD-RAD is pretty easy to detect in oneself once you know it.

THE CHILDHOOD CAUSES OF ATTACHMENT DISORDER:
- Abuse (mental, emotional, physical, sexual)
- Neglected and/or unprotected
- Abandonment
- Emotionally distant parents
- Loss of a parent due to death or divorce
- Premature birth to an incubator

- Grew up with no affection or nurturing
- Maternal depression, including in utero
- Addicted parent(s), alcohol, etc.
- Painful or major illness
- Adoption, foster care, or inconsistent day-care

ATTACHMENT DISORDER RESULTS IN ONE OR MORE OF THESE PERSONALITY TRAITS:
- Antisocial
- Narcissistic
- Obsessive-compulsive disorder (OCD)
- Dependent (feel anxiety, depression, self-judgment when single or alone; jump into relationships too fast or stay in bad ones too long)

HOW TO HEAL REACTIVE ATTACHMENT DISORDER, RAD (ONLY AN OUTLINE):
- First you have to want to heal your attachment disorder
- Realize how much it isolates, limits, and keeps you estranged from knowing a life of love
- Realize you have impact on others, especially hurtful impact
- Develop empathy (feeling how others feel)
- Develop compassion (caring about others' circumstances)
- Learn to give and receive non-sexual physical touch (affection)
- Learn to be forgiving of others
- Learn not to "ghost" friends and lovers when they disappoint or unintentionally hurt you
- Stop defending your perceived right to be angry
- Heal your misanthropy
- Let go of your addiction to your story of pain
- Heal your shame; it was given to you
- Learn to be honest, and live in a way that the truth won't be something you don't want to admit
- Be willing to bond with people by going outside of your comfort zone

- Figure out what you need and tell people
- Be willing to reach out to people
- Strive for unconditional love

*****

NARCISSISM

This disease is almost epidemic these days, so it's almost essential to become aware of it in order to have boundaries against unhealthy relationships.

The Traits of a Narcissist:

- Never accepts blame, never wrong, never apologizes
- Completely avoids answering questions that prove they're lying or wrong
- Believes they're special and unique
- Requires admiration
- Exploitive and manipulative; use people like chess pieces
- Subtly treat people like assets or possessions
- Are unable to see how others feel and don't care - others aren't really real
- Grandiose thinking
- Tell different stories to different people according to what they want them each to believe – playing them to the narcissist's own advantage
- Lie and manipulate by playing the victim card
- Lies as a habit to the point of not realizing they're lying
- Entitled and demanding
- Lack empathy
- Arrogant
- Charming when advantageous

- Choose people who make them look good and/or improve their lifestyle
- Jealous/envious. Jealousy is not having what you could have that others have; envy is not having what you can't have that others have (youth, health, good looks, talent…)
- Vicious when they don't get what they want

The US government lists narcissism as a Certified Mental Illness*!*

Narcissists are very predictable once you understand the disease. They are to be avoided (at least eventually) or at least minimized or consciously dealt with. I deal with this topic a lot in my counseling because it seems to be an epidemic in our society. (If some "only" have about seventy percent of the traits of a narcissist – a quasi-narcissist - it indicates that it's the result of having Attachment Disorder).

At one point in my life I realized I had a few narcissists in my life as "friends," but they only called me when they needed something, or, I guess I made them somehow look good. This was before I healed my Core Wound and I still had low self-esteem from "no one cares." There are exceptions to the rule, but it has become a cliché for people to believe that we only attract people in our lives that reflect back to us who we are, so I had to wonder why I had narcissists in my life since I knew I wasn't one. It was obvious I wasn't: I was always apologizing, putting others first (codependent), cared too much about what others thought of me, and cared too much about how they felt, etc.

What I realized is that I drew narcissists into my life to show me how to heal my low self-esteem. I needed to integrate some of their traits into myself in order to have normal self-esteem. You see, narcissists think too highly of themselves to a diseased level, where I thought too low of myself to a diseased level, so by learning from them through observation, I was able to consciously integrate some of their traits to bring myself up to a normal level of self-esteem.

It was a very short time after this realization that I no longer needed the "reflection" of them in my life. As they no longer resonated with me, I also chose to not have them in my life anymore, never to remain, gone. Narcissists don't care about you or, at best, pretend to (which used to fool me enough to fit my Core Wound), and "ninety-nine percent" of them never change. All they do is use you and then leave you once they have no more use for you because they've already sucked everything they can out of you, which is a great fit for a martyr, too.

***

SHAME

Most if not all of the Core Wounds are shame-based. If you read them over again, you'll see what I mean. Most of them are all different definitions of shame. Just as the adage goes that fish don't know they were born in water because it's all they know, we may not realize we're born into a culture of shame. It's compounded if you're also born into a normal dose of religion. Shame is so normal that we don't even realize we're operating within a shame-based paradigm.

If you haven't actively worked on healing shame, it is very likely you are functioning out of it and don't even know it; obviously, then, shame needs to be addressed and healed. I can introduce the relevance of the subject here, but healing it is now the exclusive focus of many books, seminars, podcasts, videos, etc.

Shame is a predominant and crucial condition to heal, and it will profoundly change your life for the better to do so. It also dovetails extremely well with healing your Core Wound. Think about it: all your Negative Ego does is shame you all the time with all its lies.

The following is a partial list of the indicators of shame. Go through it and checkmark all the ones that are true about you:

1. Do you feel unforgivable?
2. Do you get anxious when threatened by success?
3. Do you beat yourself up over little stuff?
4. Do you feel if you make a mistake, it means you are a mistake?
5. Do you get perturbed over others' success?
6. Do you feel separate and as if you don't belong?
7. Is your spirituality not as connected as you want it to be?
8. Do you feel that you can't be fixed?
9. Do you have a lot of guilt?
10. Do you feel unprepared for life?
11. Do you have anxiety?
12. Do you let other's expectations of you determine your life?
13. Do you feel like a fraud?
14. Does it give you anxiety if someone other than family says they love you?

15. Does success slip through your fingers?
16. Do you feel powerless?
17. Do you feel socially inauthentic, superficial or awkward?
18. Do you have fear of intimacy?
19. Is it difficult to form a dream for your life?
20. Do you have a hard time knowing what you want?
21. Have you found your passion, your calling?
22. Are you always dealing with pain (from the past)?
23. Are you always just getting by in life?
24. Is having integrity a struggle or unknown?
25. Do you obsess to be perfect inwardly and/or outwardly?
26. Do you fear being humiliated?
27. Were you raised by shame-based people?
28. Were you abandoned in childhood (neglect, death, divorce, shuffled around)?
29. Were you an abused child (mental, emotional, physical, sexual)?
30. Did you feel you were wronged in your childhood?
31. Is it hard for you to ask for help?
32. Do you live according to what is expected of you by others?
33. Do you enable other's unhappiness?
34. Do you shut down your emotions?
35. Is it difficult for you to receive?
36. Is it hard for you to ask for your needs to be met?
37. Do you feel anxiety when someone needs you or relies on you?
38. Are you one that never admits you're wrong?
39. Do you still have to give back the shame to those who gave it to you?
40. Do you still have to meet and "re-parent" your own Inner Child?

If you checked ten or more, you definitely have shame to heal, and that's being lenient. I wouldn't say you have to be perfect, but it'd be great to get it down to five. I also believe there is *always* constant room for improvement concerning all 40 examples. One of the main things about healing is to be persistent about it.

Like codependence, HEALING SHAME IS MANDATORY... far more so.

***

Here are three significant systems I have found very helpful in my life that would assist in healing your Core Wound. I'm certain there are many more, and I have used many more, but these stand out.

ENNEAGRAM

The enneagram is a very ancient system used to identify one's personality. It is between 4,000-4,500 years old and originated in Western Asia. It got its present name from combining the Greek word for nine (ennea) and diagram. The enneagram is a unique diagram that points out the position of nine personality types and the direction to take to evolve one's own particular personality type. It is a very accurate system, and its age is proof of its long-standing value. Awareness of the enneagram hit America sometime in the late 1970s, and this awareness is still growing. Some say it is a spiritual system, for as one works on deep self-improvement (healing), one usually becomes more authentically spiritual.

From my own experience I can attest to the enneagram's valuable healing benefits. There is a great amount of conscious power gained from realizing what type one is out of the nine on the enneagram. Each type also has a subtype, called a wing, which makes one's discoveries even more specific. Beyond the wing, there is the direction of integration to be taken, which is the map on how to evolve oneself. There is also the direction of disintegration, which is where one goes under stress when the worst of oneself comes out.

All nine types have both great attributes about themselves to work on to strengthen and also substantial shortcomings to work on to heal. Within the diagram are arrows which point to what direction to go to integrate the positive traits of another personality type and which direction to avoid going. Consciously adopting the good traits of the personality one integrates to is life-changing, as is learning to avoid taking on the not-so-great personality traits in the direction of disintegration when one is under stress and more subconsciously reactive. This path of personal growth is mapped out to proceed in a specific way for each personality type by integrating the best traits of other personality types in a precise order around the diagram. Doing this makes one's personality type the best and most whole they can be, embodying all their strengths and realizing their unique purpose in life, including being much happier and fulfilled.

Each of the nine types has a particular drive, their prime motivator. As some personality types are more fearful, others more depressed, some more courageous, some more reckless, some more angry, some more happy, some more active, etc., the enneagram gives us a specific pathway to heal any weaknesses that hold us back while also embracing traits that allow us to move forward with accumulated strengths.

The enneagram is another support system that can powerfully assist in healing your Core Wound.

***

BYRON KATIE

A woman named Byron Katie had a huge epiphany one day after having been severely depressed for ten years. A simple but extraordinarily powerful process came to her, as she suddenly had a very unassuming but profound way of healing her deepest-held unbeneficial "Twelve." Since then, Byron has given her technique to the world, which has helped an inestimable amount of people internationally, and it's just by asking yourself basically four simple questions.

Byron Katie's process applies very well to healing your Core Wound. Hopefully by now you have caught on to the voice of your Negative Ego. So, how does believing that voice make you feel? (The primary emotions of your Core Wound and their peptides you're addicted to.) And, is that voice true? You actually already know the Negative Ego's voice is a serial liar; that's all it does. And remember how it impacts your own Inner Child?

If you are so steeped in believing that voice is true because of your addiction to it, ask yourself if you know if it is absolutely true. In my case it would be, "Do I absolutely know that no one cares?" Of course not. And it's even easier to believe it's not true if you truly believe in a Higher Power. For me, just knowing I am still alive means Something (for you agnostics) cares. This same question and logic applies to anyone's Core Wound; therefore, the Core Wound is always a lie, you just have to prove it by actually reprogramming yourself.

Now that you know better, why would you hold onto a lie? Partly because you became addicted to the peptides generated by your Core Wound and the cell receptors that were created to receive those peptides, but those cellular receptors can atrophy pretty easily once you know the cause of their creation is a lie and you do something about it. Once you starve them into atrophy and experience how much your life changes, you will find it almost automatic to never feed those old cell receptors again.

As part of a large audience, I have witnessed Byron Katie's amazing and very elegant technique heal individuals' deepest issues in as little as about five to ten minutes! In Katie's work, realizing and telling yourself the truth really does set you free.

There comes a point when you can turnaround your Core Wound. For instance, though it was a deeply subconscious and dysfunctional strategy, I automatically went out of my way to show I cared for whoever was in my life, expecting they just might return caring for me as a result. I was subconsciously giving to others what I wanted to have in return. All that happened is I became codependent and a martyr. As the awareness that came from my healing, I realized I didn't have to care for or accommodate for everyone in my life, and that was ok. It was a foreign concept at first, but it was also a huge relief. Why was I the only one caring for everyone when nobody cared for me? Because it was my active Wound! I turned it around to a healthy homeostasis and healed the old automatic response.

Here are some examples of what Katie calls a turnaround for one of the Core Wounds. "There's something wrong with me (and I don't know what it is)."

- There's nothing wrong with me *because* I know what it is and am consciously healing it.
- There's something wrong with me and I know what it is and am actively working on healing it.
- There's something wrong with *them*, and I know what it is.
- There's something wrong with them, and I don't even need to know what it is.
- There's nothing wrong with me because I have a gift and am supposed to be different.

To get a glimpse of how Katie's work can be a big support to Healing Your Core Wound, here are some lines just from the introduction to her first book in 2002.[8]

"Contemporary science identifies a particular part of the brain, sometimes called "the interpreter," as the source of the familiar internal narrative that gives us our sense of self. …the left cerebral hemisphere of humans is prone to fabricating verbal narratives that do not necessarily accord to the truth… [and] weaves its story in order to convince itself… that it is in full control… having what amounts to a spin doctor in the left brain…. The interpreter is really trying to keep our personal story together. To do that, we have to learn to lie to ourselves. …[This]… explains how we get ourselves into… [our] own suffering."

The "interpreter" is our Negative Ego, the liar. It interprets reality for us based on our Core Wound, which is a lie and the source of our internal suffering and outer reactive behavior. Our Negative Ego is the spin doctor spouting off the ICOS brainwashing of our subconscious.

Your Negative Ego is the spin doctor spouting off the brainwashed ICOS.

Your Core Wound is your Identity, deeper than a belief, and your Negative Ego is the source of your limiting beliefs that spring from and support your Core Wound, which causes and perpetuates your suffering. The limiting beliefs are the lies you wrote down from your

Negative Ego that you read to your Inner Child. Byron Katie is a master at turning around and healing limiting beliefs.

The Negative Ego's lies are the limiting beliefs that spring from and support your Core Wound, and they perpetuate your suffering.

***

JIM KWIK

During the course of this writing, a client told me about Jim Kwik and his book which came out in 2020.[9] This is another excellent support to *Healing Your Core Wound.* Here are just a few quotes from his book so you can see what I mean.

"…the brain is capable of being molded and shaped, meaning that at any point anyone can decide to change the way their brain functions."

"Plasticity means that your learning, and indeed your life, is not fixed. You can be, do, have, and share anything when you optimize and rewire your brain."

"Our background and circumstances may have influenced who we are, but we must be accountable for who we become. … And when you accept that all of your potential is entirely within your control, then the power of potential grows dramatically."

"...as long as you believe your inner critic [Negative Ego] is the voice of the true... wisest you, it's always going to guide you.... But if you can create a separate persona for your inner critic... you'll be [able to quiet it]. ... Give your [Negative Ego] a preposterous name and outrageous physical attributes. Make it cartoonish and unworthy even of a B-movie. Mock it for its rigid dedication to negativity. Roll your eyes when it pops into your head. The better you become at distinguishing this voice [Negative Ego] from the real you, the better you'll be at preventing limiting beliefs from getting in your way."

Once you've neutralized or eliminated the lies, it empowers you greatly to then tell yourself the truth to fill in the void. It is in this way that you change the entire track of your life from one track of neuropathways based on negativity to an alternate track based on truth and positivity, a subconscious track versus a conscious track.

Jim Kwik also has a little drawing in his book of an iceberg, where most of it is under the surface like the subconscious. In my version of the drawing, our Core Wound would be at the very tip of the bottom of the iceberg. It is because of that drawing that a client told me about the book, plus Jim is brilliant.

CHAPTER 5
THE MOST DENIED PART OF HEALING

Mind needs to think, that's what it does; body needs to move, that's what it does; emotion needs to express, which moves mind and body, that's what it does. If emotion doesn't express, it will internalize and corrupt mind and body.

Some have asked me how long it will take to heal their Core Wound. It depends solely upon how consciously they stay aware of doing so and how strong or persistent their own willpower is. Healing it is something only they can do.

A client inspired the following: there are 365 days in a year and 360 degrees to a circle, so if you heal yourself by just one degree per day, in six months you'll be 180 degrees different from what you were, having turned your life around. The determinate then is to what average degree per day you actually heal yourself. You know what to do now, so it's up to your own willpower, which is backed by emotion.

Emotion is the missing piece almost no one ever addresses, and in my experience, emotions are the most powerful part of our being, even more than our mind. Our mind adapts to how we are feeling, even to the point of some people consciously shutting their emotions down.

Cultures around the world have historically been taught to shut emotions down. It's because emotions are so powerful that we've been taught and conditioned to not express them. Certain emotions have become so denied and judged as "unspiritual" or "bad" that all kinds of very popular teachers, workshops, books, and magazines about "spirituality" omit the word emotion entirely.

Good luck spiritually evolving or healing without addressing your emotions!

Most spiritual teachers infer – or even say - that it's somehow not spiritual to get mad or sad, or to be in fear and so on. We're taught that the most evolved people are the ones that are the least emotional, unless it's always only love, joy or peace. We're supposed to just meditate it away to "transcend our emotions" until they're basically gone so we're totally at peace, and that's called enlightenment or godly (even though, as a cultural norm, it's ok for God to have major wrath...).

People automatically assume that anger, fear, depression, and others are negative emotions, meaning that it's bad to have them or feel them, so one never should. But the only negative emotions that exist are the ones that are not expressed appropriately; appropriately is the key word. For example, love is a negative emotion if it is expressed inappropriately, and anger is a positive emotion if it is expressed appropriately. Emotions and behavior are two different things; for instance, anger is associated with bad behavior such as violence. But anger can be expressed in good ways such as firm, healthy boundaries where you won't let anything or anyone you love ever be abused, including yourself. Likewise, fear can be a positive emotion if a rattlesnake is warning you to move away, whereas most people think fear is automatically a negative emotion or, by some unchallenged logic, the opposite of love.

Emotion and behavior are two different things.

Emotions might be the most judged things on the planet, but it's because of the behaviors associated with them, not because of the actual emotion. All emotions have a positive and negative side to them according to our behavior; none of them are exclusively negative nor exclusively positive. Even shame has a positive side when it becomes remorse; true remorse can radically change one's life and one's impact on others for the better. Rather than being negative or positive, emotions merely have a higher or lower vibration and give us more energy or less energy than others, such as joy compared to sadness. One might have a good reason to be sad and a good reason to listen to the message sadness (or anger or fear, etc) has that could change one's life. It would be healthier to accept and listen to the emotion than to deny it as a negative thing and not even acknowledge or accept it, or to shame or judge one's self for even having it, as "I shouldn't feel this way...."

As a result of being taught that feeling and especially expressing emotions is not ok and that we should control them (shut them down), most have considerable shame just for having emotions, let alone expressing them, especially in public. But if we don't express our emotions, it often causes disease. Many even theorize that stuck emotions are the cause of all disease. We know emotions cause chemicals within our body (peptides), and if we let emotions fester in us by denying we have them or don't healthily express them or shut them down, this theory makes sense. Personally, I think it's true and not just a theory.

I had tons of rage from my very unfair and highly abusive childhood, and I suppressed it by drinking alcohol, starting at age twelve. Once I stopped drinking, all that suppressed rage could no longer be contained, starting at age thirty-one. I was led to those remarkably powerful five-day emotional-release workshops where I learned how to express it safely and at maximum levels. The chemical of rage literally sweat out of my body; it collected on my armpit hair (yeah, I know...) and crystalized. I had to shave it off my armpits because it wouldn't even wash off with a scrubber. I learned later that it was uric acid, and that uric acid crystalizes *within* one's body like it did on the outside of my body, and it causes all kinds of havoc, especially joint pain, and that uric acid is caused by drinking too much alcohol.

It turns out that uric acid becomes the "N-terminal pro-B-type natriuretic **peptide**." I would say that, for me, as my subconscious caused the psychological/emotional desire to drink, and my rage fueled that desire (from the ICOS I received growing up with raging alcoholics), and as alcohol was the physical supply of the peptide, the way I soothed my rage was to be addicted to alcohol, as it continuously maintained the quenching of cell receptors all along my neuropathways throughout my brain and body. (That's another way of saying I wasn't angry when I drank but was angry or depressed when I didn't.) This is the function of a self-sustaining positive feedback loop (remember, a positive feedback loop's a bad thing). Drinking helped me *harbor* rage rather than let it go. It helped me cope with my rage the only way I knew how, until I chose to heal and became conscious and willing enough to find how to release rage in a healthy way. "Drinking rage" had been causing major disease within me while also causing my "Twelve" to be unhealthy.

Rage and alcohol actually killed my mother, who drank and expressed rage *every night*, but instead of letting it go she harbored it to use the next night, continually, literally for decades. Ultimately, it caused gout that moved throughout her body, bursitis, huge cysts on her kidneys, and a largely swollen liver, etc. Plus her Negative Ego fully took over her "Twelve" in a complete, chronic Negative Ego Brain Storm until her Core Wound ("I'm not in charge of my own life") literally killed her.

For our healing, we must acknowledge, accept, and listen to our emotions and find healthy ways to express them instead of harboring them or feeling guilty or numb about them, so that they won't cause damage upon our mind, body, and spirit and the lives of others.

And then there's the affect that denying emotion has on our passion. Emotions are where our passion and willpower originate. It's not even "what if" all our emotions are part of what prepares us for passion to find us; they are. Why do you think so many people don't have any passion? So many are lost and don't have any clue as to what they want to do with their lives because they've shut down their emotions or don't know what to do with them. Emotions help us become clear about things if we express them cleanly, safely, and without guilt.

Emotions help us become clear about things if we express them cleanly, safely, and without guilt.

Mahatma Gandhi is a great example of how emotion leads to passion or life purpose. As an adult, he was a lawyer full of rage at all the brutal abuse and injustice the British were perpetrating upon the populace of his country of India for at least one-hundred years during and before the official British rule of 1858-1947. His rage was the spark that started his passion and destiny in life and had major impact upon the world. So how is rage a negative emotion when even Gandi started with it and became known as one of the most spiritual people in history? It's what you do with it which makes it either negative or positive!

Sometimes some of us need anger to fire us up, and that's what passion is: fire. What happens if we automatically judge certain emotions as bad? We set ourselves up for never finding our passion.

It's not just anger that can motivate passion, but also fear, love, and grief, etc., too.

Every emotion we have is a messenger and is there for a reason, so I always encourage people to pay attention to, feel, and find a way to express their emotions. In the case of your Core Wound, you now know that the primary emotions that are connected to your Wound indicate to you when your Negative Ego/Liar is talking to you inside your head. Your Negative Ego has been in charge of your subconscious for decades; it got you addicted to "your favorite worst feelings," which became your dysfunctional comfort zone, the one you've known since your programming as a child.

We became chemically addicted to the comfort zone of our Core Wound. This is literally true because every emotion we have creates a peptide, a molecular chemical, which enters our bloodstream and crosses our blood-brain barrier. These peptides attach to cells throughout our body but particularly to cells in our brain, our guts, and our heart. Our cells have adapted to receive these steady supply of peptides, and our cells create more receptors to generate the capacity to accommodate more peptides. When the receptors don't get enough of their supply, our body, mind, and emotion need a "fix," so, one way or another, we create the familiar circumstances in our life from our ICOS/Template, generated by our "Twelve," in order to get our "fix." This is known as self-sabotage. Those urgings are for more of the peptides that fulfill the feelings of our Core Wound. We become addicted to "our favorite worst feelings," such as self-pity, depression, anger, sadness, anxiety, loneliness, or an array of others that sustain any of the Core Wounds. Self-sabotage keeps us in our comfort zone, our familiar.

Out of all the five Kingdoms of Life, mammals, as a small part of the Animal Kingdom, are the only life forms on Earth that have a limbic brain (reptiles have traces of the beginnings of one). Though it has many functions, of course, our limbic brain is the part of our brain which generates our ability to have emotions. As our emotions cause peptides (and vice-versa) that flow into our brain, our thinking (and our "Twelve") is accordingly affected. Yet it is the ability (and necessity) of our neocortex to bring consciousness to our subconscious limbic, emotional system rather than allowing it to always be reactive and constantly regenerating our Core Wound's "Twelve." It is already possible and readily available to consciously wean ourselves off the peptides of our Core Wound's emotional comfort zone – our familiar - and replace them with peptides that are a result of conscious awareness and choice. When that happens, the former peptide receptors along the neuropathways of one's Core Wound begin to atrophy and wither away to never again beg for their "fix."

My point for bringing all this up is to say that you need to include your emotions so they are on the same team with your mind, body, and spirit to all work together on your mission of healing. You don't want to leave emotion out of the mission because you will probably fail or take forever. It will greatly enhance your healing to become conscious of and accept your emotions rather than push them away, remain in denial of them, or forever ruminate over them to harbor them. This is because the aspects of any subconscious, reactive emotions that especially come from your Negative Ego will cause you to relapse and set you back perhaps several degrees. More so, they will cause toxic thoughts and behavior, which also cause toxic chemicals to manifest in your body, and you can't just think those chemicals out of your body. That's like lying in bed thinking about working out at the gym and believing that will get you in shape. My point is you have to move those emotional peptide chemicals out of your body.

The peptides of your Core Wound must be moved out of your body with emotional and physical movement.

I think of emotions as magnetic; they tend to stick within us if we don't let them flow. They create neuropathways of their own we could call Memory Lane (connected to our limbic brain's hippocampus) and cause their own peptides, the original chemical communication system within all lifeforms, which was genetically built into us.

So how do we release toxic peptides out of our body? All these peptides are associated with the limiting beliefs our Negative Ego/Liar tells us in order to perpetuate our Core Wound/Lie. A lot of clients tell me they release their anger at the gym, but that doesn't work. It releases "steam," yes, but the pressure cooker's still cooking. Releasing our emotions is all about intention; intention adds consciousness. Just aggressively working out at the gym is rarely ever done with intention about healing a Core Wound issue; it's usually a reaction as a way to release "steam" because you don't know what else to do to unplug the pressure cooker altogether.

For me, releasing emotion with intention has always been a blast. It's fun because it works, which makes it very rewarding; life opens up, our brain opens up, clarity appears, and life becomes easier, less painful, and more free. There are so many ways to do it, and it's all very basic.

There are plenty of rocks when you go outdoors into the woods, an ocean beach, or in a wild lightning storm, etc. Sandstone is great to work with if it's available. You want to find a thin rock about the size of a sand-dollar or less, and then imagine who or what issue this thin rock represents (Negative Ego, ex-spouse, mother, father, Core Wound, etc.). Lay it on a hard surface then find a bigger rock to throw with both hands to smash it with (do not hold on to it, so you don't smash your fingers), as this bigger rock represents a pattern you want to break at the same time as you're vaporizing the issue you've identified (smaller rock).

I'd say one-hundred percent of the clients I've seen have never done anything like this, and they've all loved it. You never know how good it feels until you do it. What have you always wanted to tell your abusive step-father, your cheating ex, your backstabbing co-worker or some "unforgiveable" thing you've done? What issues do you have with them? Here's your chance to let one of them have it and give it your all (at "full volume") plus break the pattern you've had that held the dynamic of pain in place you've had with them. Some people don't want to quit once they've finally had permission to let it rip! It makes all the difference to give it intention, to consciously identify the issue and the pattern you want to break.

Again, there are so many ways to do it, but I encourage you to be physical and emotional about it. I learned to beat the daylights out of pillows; it didn't hurt me or anyone else. One of the best or most worthwhile times I ever spent healing started off with what was supposed to be a one-hour private session with one of the emotional release guides from those workshops I attended. It was about my mother, and it turned into a four-hour session of moving tons of emotional energy. I got so much poison out of me in those four hours that I healed the vast majority of my mother issues for life along with whatever that poison would have done to me if I'd have let it stay in me. I went so hard at it I even threw up. Getting that kind of emotional intensity out of me was a dream come true and healed a major chunk of my life and changed me forever. After that, I also found I had cleared out enough room within me to be grateful and forgive her. In turn, though I didn't know it at the time, that very day strongly reinforced and accelerated the new neuropathways I had already begun that led and contributed to ultimately turning my life around to joy.

Don't bypass doing something like this. Anger has neuropathways throughout our body not just our brain, pathways that make anger want to physically strike out. So maybe take a "baseball bat to a punching bag," somehow, with a stick figure duct-taped to it of someone you have issues with that still stick in you. You don't want to have to stop once you have finally created the rare time and space and willpower to move your energy this way; don't waste the opportunity. (That's why that one-hour session I just mentioned turned into four).

Another option, perhaps, is to use a tennis racket to beat the crap out of a mattress or couch... with a little ragdoll or something that represents who or what the issue is. Or get a bunch of tennis balls and "serve" them with intention at an intentional target (like a cardboard cut-out of someone you have issues with) in the garage, barn or wherever, vocalizing yourself. Let'er rip. Get it out of you. Do it in private. Be creative. And don't just write a hate letter and burn it because that's mostly mental.

Be responsible for your emotions and quit dumping them onto others or expressing them inappropriately. Don't hurt yourself or anybody else. Be clean about it. Don't destroy others' property, etc. This is about intentional healing and letting go. It's healthy anger by admitting the truth and getting it out of you. No one else ever even needs to know if you don't want. It's called independent resolution. It brings a ton of clarity that you can't even imagine until you've done it. And it sets you free. Guilt or shame is all that's holding you back from at *least* expressing this for yourself. It's way better than getting and staying sick while paying for all those doctor bills if you never do it.

Though I've used anger as an example, you can do this with any of the primary emotions you identified that are connected to your Core Wound. Who gave you your unworthiness? Who gave you your shame? Or your anxiety, your sadness, your unsafety, etc? Let'em have it and get it out of you. Give it back to them. Heal your Core Wound and get your passion back; bring yourself back to life and quit leading a mediocre life based on pain or denial or buried victimhood or guilt or shame.

Basically, it's just admitting your core emotional truth without guilt. You take a shower every day to clean your physical being, but when have you ever cleansed your emotional being? If not, you have no clue how refreshing it feels nor the clarity it will give you. Otherwise, you're free to contract ailments in your body, mind, emotions and spirit.

I've found an immense amount of fun, benefit, and relief getting used to being uncomfortable (all healing's outside your comfort zone). A lot of things can't just be thought away, as you probably already know. And there are emotional toxins (like uric acid) and many other peptides that must be worked out of your lymphatic system, your joints, your internal organs, including your brain, and it takes emotional, physical movement.

I told you I didn't heal my Core Wound through conventional means, but nonetheless, emotions are the most denied part of our existence, and our emotional nature needs to be addressed. "Resistance is futile" to doing emotional release if you really want to heal. Find your way of doing it. Learn to identify your emotions, discover where they come from, own them, move them, and be responsible in the way you do so. Do it to heal your Core Wound; do it to create new neuropathways with consciously created peptides; do it to create a new "Twelve"; do it for your Inner Child; do it for clarity and to get unstuck; do it to heal your guilt; do it to realize your passion and find why you're really here. Do it to become fully alive and on fire!

Remember, one of the aspects of the "Twelve" is perspective. Healing your Core Wound will change your emotions, which will drastically change your perspective about life. Your new healthier emotions will support your new neuropathways with new emotional peptides that support your new emotions… you'll never go back to how you were because both your brain pattern and your brain chemistry will be permanently changed for the better.

***

COMMITMENT CEREMONY

By now you know how to clear out what needs to be cleared out of your mind, emotions, and body. You're ready to further your ability to consciously create your own reality rather than to keep hoarding all that dusty old pain and toxic memories up in the attic or down in the basement of your subconscious mind and your body. You can now add some rocket fuel to your newly created, budding neuropathways throughout your being and heal your spirit - and connect to Spirit much better.

That rocket fuel is described by the most powerful word in our language, a word that I know has the power to change your life instantly, depending on how much you mean it. The word commit is the most powerful word in our language.

For instance, some may say love is the most powerful word, but one must commit to love first. A true commitment will change your life (committing to marriage, having kids, college, joining the military, etc.) Commitment is where consciousness and willpower come into play. We can amplify our choices and willpower with commitment. Commitment is what turns a dream into reality (and the subconscious isn't going to do it). After your commitment, it's either yes or no from thereon; your thoughts, attitude and behavior are either supporting your commitment or not.

The word <u>commit</u> is the most powerful word in our language.

It's time for a Commitment Ceremony whenever you're ready. In fact, you cannot do one until you truly are ready. This is a commitment to yourself, and you can't fool yourself, so you have to mean it, and you have to be ready to make it real. And you have to do it with emotion, however that comes out for you, as long as it's concentrated and authentic. Because I've done it, I can guarantee you the emotion of true commitment creates its own beneficial peptides that can light up your entire brain, body, spirit, and Soul enough to cause permanent change.

Since this type of commitment is for one's self, I've always done it alone (though it's also great to have a witness), usually out in the woods. I like to yell it at full volume because it's how much my willpower means it, it's more fun for me, and my Inner Child loves it. I yell it also because I don't care who hears it because you kind of want to publicize it anyway. You want anyone in the world to know your commitment. You want to metaphorically put it in the New York Times Public Notices.

I do them one at a time and not until any prior one is already sufficiently integrated into my life. If you're going to do this out in the woods (ocean beach, lightning storm, etc.), pick up a good-sized rock so it's not too heavy but fairly heavy. You are going to use this rock as an exclamation point. Be safe about it; after all, you don't want to hurt yourself since this is a gift of self-love. Also be present with it; you're doing this with conscious intention. Do such commitments one at a time, even if months or years go by in between. They'll be one of the greatest gifts you ever give yourself.

Choose your time and place, choose what you're going to commit to, express it out loud to the core of your being, and then smash that rock to bits to show how much you mean it as an exclamation point. This is my own way of usually doing it, but it is only a suggestion, though I have had plenty of clients that have fully loved it, to say the least.

So… keep your commitment statement down to four to seven words. It is meant to be a power punch not a long description or lecture to yourself that you won't even remember. For instance, when I made my first commitment I already knew it meant giving and receiving affection, so I didn't need to say, "I commit to giving and receiving affection!" I found it much more potent to express it as, "I COMMIT TO AFFECTION!"

Here is a list of suggestions:

I commit to healing my Core Wound!

I commit to healing my Inner Child!

I commit to forgiving!

I commit to being valued!

I commit to creating healthy boundaries!

I commit to healing my rage!

I commit to being loved!

I commit to being confident!

I commit to healthy communication!

I commit to healthy relationships!

I commit to speaking up for myself!

I commit to freedom!

I commit to unconditional love!

I commit to healing my reactive behavior!

I commit to actualizing my Higher Self!

I commit to creating safety!

I commit to healing shame!

I commit to healing codependency!

The word commit is the most powerful because after you make a genuine commitment, your thoughts, feelings, and behavior become a yes or a no, period. Does this thought, feeling or behavior support my commitment or not? If the answer is no, I immediately change whichever thought, feeling or behavior I'm doing, so I'm rarely off track and never for long - like minutes or less.

I never thought the following would be possible, and it took years before I unexpectedly realized I was ready, but it worked instantly and the result has never gone away:

I commit to joy!

I call it a transcendent joy, joy without denial, because I still feel everything else when it comes up, but I feel everything else within the backdrop of joy and feel it for joy's sake without staying in the "heavier" emotions too long... but as long as needed.

Yes, I literally yell my commitments to and from the mountaintops at full volume, and I don't care who hears it. I would take it to heart if I were to hear such an unforgettable statement coming out of nowhere...

THE WORLD AWAITS YOUR HEALING.

AFTERWORD

If you haven't yet come to unconditionally loving your Inner Child, nor they unconditionally loving you, their Future Self, how are you going to receive the love you've always wished for from somebody else? How are you going to love your Future Self from the continual Present Self from now on? Is your Future Self going to be your hero from now on as you (hopefully) are to your Inner Child? Is your Future Self loving you from a brilliant future they've created for you? How is your Future Self loving you from the future if you're not even loving your Inner Child as their Future Self in the present? Are you currently receiving the love your Higher Self and Soul have for you? All of them, including your Inner Child, can help guide you to a future of health and an unconditional, joyous love of life. Your Core Wound is the biggest blockage of all to attaining any of that.

***

Humanity at large also has a Core Wound. I would venture to say that it is: "We are on our own." As with any Core Wound, it is also a lie. We have all of the amazing creations of life all around us and are connected to every lifeform on Earth through the fundamental DNA we all share in common. But, just as we do individually, if we don't heal our collective Core Wound, we will end up proving, by our own actions, that "we are on our own." If we continue to believe what we've been subconsciously taught by our culture - that we are separate from or above Nature or that Nature is our enemy, for instance - such beliefs from our collective cultural Wound will forever haunt our future, as we continue to soon send eventually millions of nonhuman species into extinction. In a very real sense, our species (at least the dominant, nonindigenous culture) has Attachment Disorder relative to all the other life on Earth.

Healing our own Core Wound is how we begin to heal the collective.

Bibliography of Notations

1. Sedona Soul Adventures. Sedona, AZ: sedonasouladventures.com (Rated one of the top eleven spiritual/couples retreats in the world (2022), rated #1 in the United States in 2015-2023, winner of Best Retreats in Sedona since inception of the Award, and many more.)
2. Nadine Burke Harris, M.D. *The Deepest Well: Healing the Long-Term Effects of Childhood Trauma and Adversity.* New York, NY: HarperCollins Publishers, 2018. (This is a brilliant must-read full of groundbreaking research.)
3. Brown, Dan. *Origin.* New York: Doubleday, a division of Penguin Random House LLC, 2017.
4. Lazaris. *The New Millennium with Lazaris.* Orlando, FL: NPN Publishing, 1999.
5. Walsch, Neale Donald. *Conversations With God: An Uncommon Dialogue, Book 1.* New York, NY: G. P. Putnam's Sons, 1996.
6. Pert, Candace. *The Molecules of Emotion.* New York, NY: Scribner/Simon & Schuster, 1997.
7. Hogsett, Jesse. De-Tached: Surviving Reactive Attachment Disorder. Modesto, CA: JH Publishing, 2011.
8. Katie, Byron. *Loving What Is: Four Questions That Can Change Your Life.* New York, NY: Harmony Books, a division of Penguin Random House LLC, 2002.
9. Kwik, Jim. Limitless: Upgrade Your Brain, Learn Anything Faster, and Unlock Your Exceptional Life. Carlsbad, CA: Hay House, Inc, 2020.

Acknowledgements

Special gratitude goes out to the extraordinarily healing friendship of Lazaris, a consciousness that permeates this book and has been profoundly healing in my life; the Earth Living Foundation and their life-changing emotional-release workshops (in Mexico now); Ceanne DeRohan, author; all of the non-mainstream healers I've experienced, especially Jeannie Krieder, MD (Bellevue, WA); Native American culture for teaching me more than I can say; and the spirit of my Great Grandma Alice. Kudos to my family of origin who fulfilled their Soul Contract with me to wound me perfectly as planned (a positive belief I've chosen). To all my relations and the lessons and healing given, intentionally or not; I am entirely grateful to all of you.

Special thanks to Debra Stangl, founder/owner of Sedona Soul Adventures, a many-times and highly awarded Spiritual Retreat Center, for creating such an elegant platform for my specialty to develop as an independent contractor. Sincere gratitude to the very skillful team who've done all the incredible number of complexities to have always kept the functions of the business going so well! In memory of Mona Ponce, so sweet, who also came up with the last Core Wound within the list, not one I would have thought of, now one of her gifts to the world.

I am especially grateful to all the clients I have seen, all of whom have contributed to the evolution of this work. I honor you for choosing to heal, your lives all amaze me, and you have all taught and changed me, too. My heart goes out to you, and this book would not have developed without you.

About the Author

The website, healcorewound.com, is where one may find more information about this book and connections to social media. In-person workshops, online seminars, and a monthly online support subscription are in constant development. A training program to become a professional Certified Core Wound Counselor© or Certified Core Wound Coach© are also being constantly upgraded. Obviously, one of the top qualifications is to have sufficiently proven you have healed your own Core Wound. Neuroplasticity may sound like a big, complicated word; however, the ability to consciously create new neuropathways that entirely change one's brain pattern and brain chemistry is easier than ever here. It is up to your own consciousness and willpower now. A new life certainly awaits you, and a great new career or a potent addition to your own current counseling or coaching also awaits you as well if such is your calling.

The author has forever found solace and beauty in nature. His naturalist love of life on Earth prompted him to publish his first book, *Forsaken Earth the Ongoing Mass Extinction*, in 2016 (Lulu Press/lulu.com). Though he has a wide variety of interests, his dedication to healing finds him continuing to counsel people in the midst of the exceptional scenery of Sedona, as he works on his next book on healing Attachment Disorder.

Printed in Great Britain
by Amazon

58522441R00091